Developing Listening Skills 3

Second Edition

3

Casey Malarcher

Developing Listening Skills 3 Second Edition

Casey Malarcher

© 2010 Compass Publishing

Acquisitions Editor: John Thomas
Illustrator: Hieram Weintraub
Design: Design Plus

email: info@compasspub.com
http://www.compasspub.com

ISBN: 978-1-59966-528-3

18 17 16 15 14 13 12 11 10
17 16 15 14

Photo Credits

All images © Shutterstock, Inc.
except: pp. 24, 44, 92, 102, 114, 144 © iStock International Inc.

Printed in Korea

CONTENTS

36 Topics of *Developing Listening Skills, Second Edition*

UNIT	BOOK 1	BOOK 2	BOOK 3
UNIT 1	First Meeting	Entertainment	Locations
UNIT 2	Family and Friends	Shopping	Promises
UNIT 3	Free Time	Work	Special Occasions
UNIT 4	Date and Time	Computers	Steps and Plans
UNIT 5	Telephone	Travel	Music
UNIT 6	Directions	Restaurants	Groups
UNIT 7	Schools	Hotels	Outdoors
UNIT 8	Sports	Transportation	Meetings
UNIT 9	Appearance	Banks	Feelings
UNIT 10	Weather	Driving	Favors
UNIT 11	Instructions	Housing	Memories
UNIT 12	Stories	Health	Assistance

Locations

Warm-up

A
Look & Listen

Listen to the dialogs. Write the number in the room where the speakers are. ((« Track 1 »))

A

B

C

D

B
Listen Again

Listen again, and fill in the note diagram with information from the dialogs. ((« Track 2 »))

Where?	What?	Location?
1. _____	_____	beside the _____ / on the _____
2. _____	_____	in the _____ / next to the _____
3. _____	_____ / _____	under the _____ in the _____ / above the _____
4. _____	_____	in Brenda's _____ / by the _____

C
Essential Expressions

In your notebook, draw the following shapes in the correct place.

1. a circle inside a square
2. a triangle on a square
3. a diamond next to a circle
4. a square under a diamond

5. a triangle above a circle
6. a diamond beside a triangle
7. a square behind a circle
8. a circle between two diamonds

Listening Practice

A

How would you answer?

Listen. Write the answer. ((Track 3))

Inside the closet by the front door.   No, let's put them on the piano.
Not much. Just a big tree.   Not that I could see.   That's a wonderful idea.

1. _____
2. _____
3. _____
4. _____
5. _____

B

How would you ask?

Listen. Write the question. ((Track 4))

What's the matter?   Did you put up the pictures I gave you?
Which picnic table should we use?   Where do you keep your photo albums?
         Why are there crayons all around the room?

1. _____
2. _____
3. _____
4. _____
5. _____

C

Picture Description

Describe the picture using the words below.

| in the cupboard | on the counter |
| next to the plate | above the table |

_____
_____
_____
_____
_____

✓ **Listen to the description of the picture.** ((Track 5))

Speaking Practice

A

Intonation Practice

In certain four-syllable statements or questions, the stress should be on the first and last syllables. Say the following statements and questions using the stress pattern "da dum dum da."

Written	Spoken
1. It is not in there.	1. **It's** not in **there**.
2. Look on your desk.	2. **Look** on your **desk**.
3. They're are in her purse.	3. **They're** in her **purse**.

✓ **Now practice saying the following sentences. Remember to stress the first and last syllables.**

1. Let's put it here.
2. They're on the chair.
3. She's in the car.

✓ **Now listen and repeat.** ((Track 6))

B

Conversation Pictures

Listen to the dialogs, and number the pictures. ((Track 7))

✓ **Now listen to the dialogs again, and choose the correct location.**

1. (A) above   (B) near   (C) outside   (D) beside
2. (A) above   (B) near   (C) outside   (D) beside
3. (A) above   (B) near   (C) outside   (D) beside
4. (A) above   (B) near   (C) outside   (D) beside

Short Dialogs

A

Dialog 1

Listen to the dialog and questions. Choose the best answer. ((Track 8))

1. (A) At a hotel   (B) Beside the pool
   (C) In the garage   (D) In the house

2. (A) A police officer   (B) An employee
   (C) Her husband   (D) Madam Humphrey

✓ **Listen again, and fill in the blanks.**

M: The book said that Madam Humphrey was lying near the
   ❶_____ when the detective found the body.

W: Who do you think ❷_____ her?

M: I think the maid did it. She was standing ❸_____
   the body when Madam Humphrey's husband
   ❹_____.

W: That sounds strange. I wonder why the maid would kill her.

M: Maybe her boss knew some dark ❺_____ from
   the maid's past.

W: Do you think that secret might have something to do with
   the clue that was found on the ❻_____?

M: That's probably a good ❼_____.

W: We'll just have to keep ❽_____ until we find out.

B

Dialog 2

Listen to the dialog and questions. Choose the best answer. ((Track 9))

1. (A) A cabinet   (B) A closet
   (C) A desk   (D) A table

2. (A) A bed   (B) A box
   (C) School supplies   (D) Some books

C

Dialog 3

Listen to the dialog, and choose the right phrase to complete each sentence. ((Track 10))

1. The woman is showing her friend (around her home / inside her office).
2. There is a nice view of the park (from the roof / through a window).

Main Dialog

Listen to the dialog, and choose the best answer. ((Track 11))

1. What is the man looking for?
   - (A) His father's keys
   - (B) His keys
   - (C) His mother's keys
   - (D) His sister's keys

2. Where did he not check?
   - (A) On the bookshelf
   - (B) On the piano
   - (C) Under the bed
   - (D) Under the couch

3. In which room should the keys be kept?
   - (A) The bedroom
   - (B) The garage
   - (C) The kitchen
   - (D) The living room

Listen again, and fill in the blanks. ((Track 12))

W: What are you doing with those ❶_____ cushions?

M: I'm looking for something.

W: Uh oh. What did you lose this time?

M: ❷_____ car keys. I've looked everywhere, but I can't find them!

W: You used the car last ❸_____, didn't you? What did you do with the ❹_____ after you got home?

M: I thought I put them on the ❺_____ in the living room, but they're not there.

W: Did you look under the ❻_____?

M: Yes, and I felt on top of the ❼_____ in the living room, too!

W: Well, how about inside your ❽_____? Maybe you should check the pockets of the ❾_____ that you were wearing last night.

M: I bet you're right. I was really ❿_____ when I got home, so I probably forgot to take them ⓫_____ my pocket. Here they are!

W: You should hang them on the key hook in the ⓬_____ before they get lost again.

Short Talks

Listen to the short talk and questions. Choose the best answer. ((Track 13))

1. (A) A job
   (B) A trunk
   (C) Her car
   (D) Her shoes

2. (A) In her bedroom
   (B) In the dining room
   (C) In the garage
   (D) In the kitchen

✓ **Listen again, and fill in the blanks.**

I always seem to have a hard time remembering where I ❶_____ my things. For example, the other day I was getting ready for a job ❷_____, but I couldn't find the ❸_____ I was planning to wear with my business suit. I looked in my ❹_____ and by the front door and even under the couch in the ❺_____ room. My shoes were nowhere to be found. Then my ❻_____ reminded me that I had left them in the ❼_____ of the car after I got one of them repaired. Sure enough, there they were. It's a good thing my mother has a better ❽_____ than I do.

Listen to the short talk and questions. Choose the best answer. ((Track 14))

1. (A) Birds
   (B) Flowers
   (C) Neighbors
   (D) Trees

2. (A) Spring
   (B) Summer
   (C) Fall
   (D) Winter

Listen to the short talk, and check (✓) the things the speaker describes. ((Track 15))

- ☐ a sugar bowl
- ☐ a tea pot
- ☐ dresses
- ☐ musicians
- ☐ servants
- ☐ tea cups

Listening Quiz

A

Picture Matching

Listen to the dialogs. Choose the correct picture. ((Track 16))

 **A**

 **B**

 **C**

1. (A)   (B)   (C)

2. (A)   (B)   (C)

B

Listen & Choose

Listen to the dialogs and questions. Choose the best answer. ((Track 17))

3. (A) The remote
   (C) The television

   (B) The sofa
   (D) The television guide

4. (A) Paint
   (C) Pots

   (B) Pictures
   (D) Wallpaper

5. (A) His wife
   (C) Sally

   (B) Megan
   (D) The woman

6. (A) The man
   (C) Both of them

   (B) The woman
   (D) Neither of them

7. (A) Under the bed
   (C) In the closet

   (B) Beside the clothes hamper
   (D) On the table

8. (A) Behind the dog's house
   (C) Inside the house

   (B) In the neighbor's yard
   (D) Under the stairs

9. (A) Behind the dog's house
   (C) Inside the house

   (B) In the neighbor's yard
   (D) Under the stairs

A

Pre-listening
Discussion

B

Listening
Comprehension

C

Dictation
Practice

Talk about these questions.

1. How many rooms does a typical apartment have?
2. Do small apartments in your country have special names?
3. What do you think the words "efficient" or "efficiency" mean?

Listen and answer the questions. ((Track 18))

1. **What do most people who get efficiency apartments use for beds?**

   _____.

2. **What are two differences between a studio apartment and an efficiency apartment?**

   _____.

3. **Why do artists prefer to live in lofts?**

   _____.

Listen again, and fill in the blanks. ((Track 19))

When a **1**_____ person starts **2**_____ or moves **3**_____ a new
4_____ for his **5**____ her first **6**_____, it is **7**_____ for him or **8**_____
to rent **9**____ apartment rather **10**_____ buy a **11**_____. For those **12**_____
can't afford **13**_____ apartments, there **14**_____ certain kinds **15**____ smaller
apartments **16**_____ are cheaper **17**____ rent. These **18**_____ apartments
19_____ be called **20**_____ apartments, studio **21**_____, or lofts.
     22____ efficiency is **23**_____ an apartment **24**_____ has only **25**_____
room. The **26**_____ living in **27**_____ an apartment **28**_____, cooks, and
29_____ in the **30**_____ room! For **31**_____ reason, most **32**_____
who move **33**_____ efficiency apartments **34**_____ couches that **35**____
turn into **36**_____. That way, **37**_____ the day **38**_____ can sit **39**____
the couch **40**____ read or **41**_____ TV. Then **42**____ night, he **43**____ she will
44_____ the couch **45**_____ a bed **46**_____ sleep on **47**____.
     By comparison, **48**____ studio apartment **49**____ usually larger **50**_____ an
efficiency. **51**_____, a studio **52**_____ is still **53**____ apartment
with **54**_____ a single **55**_____ space. In **56**_____ to being **57**_____, a
studio **58**_____ also have **59**____ better kitchen **60**_____ a cheaper **61**_____
apartment. For **62**_____, where an **63**_____ might have **64**_____
a small **65**_____ with a **66**_____ and small **67**_____ range next
68____ it, a **69**_____ could include **70**____ stove under **71**_____ cooking range.
     72____ loft can **73**_____ renters with **74**_____ largest living **75**____ of
these **76**_____ types of **77**_____. Originally, lofts **78**_____ empty
floors **79**_____ old warehouses **80**_____ people changed **81**_____ living
spaces. **82**_____ liked living **83**____ these kinds **84**____ places because **85**_____
spaces were **86**_____ and there **87**_____ plenty of **88**_____ to be
89_____ in such **90**____ living space. **91**_____ in a **92**_____ large loft,
93_____ are no **94**_____ dividing up **95**_____ living space. **96**_____ only
walls **97**_____ a loft **98**_____ usually found **99**_____ the bathroom.

Listening Test 🕘

PART I: Picture Description ((Track 20))

Listen and choose the statement that best describes what you see in the picture.

1.

    (A)   (B)   (C)   (D)

2.

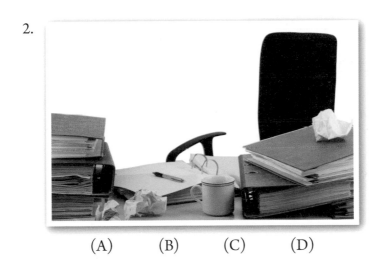

    (A)   (B)   (C)   (D)

3.

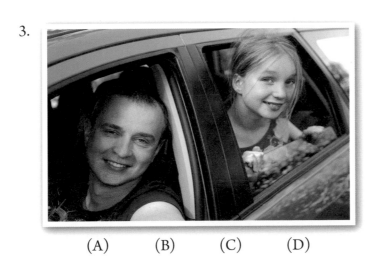

    (A)   (B)   (C)   (D)

4.

(A)   (B)   (C)   (D)

5.

(A)   (B)   (C)   (D)

PART II: Questions and Responses (« Track 21 »)

Listen and choose the best response to each question.

6. (A)   (B)   (C)

7. (A)   (B)   (C)

8. (A)   (B)   (C)

9. (A)   (B)   (C)

10. (A)   (B)   (C)

PART III: Short Conversations ((Track 22))

You will hear two dialogs, each followed by three questions. Listen carefully, and choose the best answer to each question.

11. What's on the first floor?

    (A) The man's laundry room
    (B) The man's car
    (C) The man's apartment
    (D) The man's neighbor

12. How does the woman get to the laundromat?

    (A) She rides her bike.
    (B) She drives.
    (C) She runs.
    (D) She takes the bus.

13. Where is the woman's laundromat?

    (A) Inside her apartment
    (B) On the first floor
    (C) A few blocks away
    (D) To the right

---

14. What was the man looking for?

    (A) His magazine
    (B) His running shoes
    (C) His coffee
    (D) His keys

15. Where did he look twice?

    (A) In his backpack
    (B) On the coffee table
    (C) In the closet
    (D) In the magazine

16. Where did he find the keys?

    (A) Under a magazine
    (B) Under the coffee table
    (C) Inside his backpack
    (D) In his pocket

PART IV: Short Talks ((Track 23))

You will hear two talks, each followed by three questions. Listen carefully, and choose the best answer to each question.

17. Which room does the speaker describe?

   (A) The bedroom
   (B) The living room
   (C) The kitchen
   (D) The bathroom

18. What is on the wall?

   (A) A large painting
   (B) A bookcase
   (C) An entertainment center
   (D) A shelf with a mirror

19. Why does the speaker love this room?

   (A) Because she can watch TV
   (B) Because it is relaxing
   (C) Because she loves the beach
   (D) Because it is very bright

---

20. Where is The View located?

   (A) Between the police station and the bank
   (B) Between the museum and the parking garage
   (C) Between the bank and the museum
   (D) Between the parking garage and the police station

21. What comes with each unit?

   (A) A kitchen and a washer and dryer
   (B) A private gym and large bedrooms
   (C) Free parking and laundry service
   (D) A nice view of the river

22. Where is the private gym located?

   (A) Underground
   (B) 1st floor
   (C) 12th floor
   (D) Near the main office

UNIT 2 Promises

Warm-up

A
Look & Listen

Listen to the dialogs. Write the number next to the speakers. ((Track 24))

B
Listen Again

Listen again, and fill in the blanks. ((Track 25))

1. The boy guarantees _____.
2. The girl promises _____.
3. The boy promises _____.
4. The girl promises _____.

C
Essential Expressions

Circle the best word or phrase to complete each sentence.

1. What can you say as part of a promise?
   (A) "You have my word of honor."   (B) "You have to swear."

2. How can you make a promise to a friend?
   (A) By saying, "I break my word"   (B) By saying, "I cross my heart"

3. What does a company do when they say they will fix a product for free?
   (A) Guarantee it   (B) Swear that it is good

4. When your friend believes you, what might he or she say?
   (A) "I'll keep my promise."   (B) "OK, if you say so."

5. What does a new president do?
   (A) Make a marriage vow   (B) Take an oath of office

Listening Practice

How would you answer?

Listen. Write the answer. ((Track 26))

I don't recall making any such promise.	I promise I won't lose it.
If you say so, then I believe you.	I swear I won't tell anyone.
You have my word of honor.	

1. _____
2. _____
3. _____
4. _____
5. _____

B

How would you ask?

Listen. Write the question. ((Track 27))

Are you sure I'm going to like the food here?
Do you cross your heart and hope to die?
Do you swear that you never saw it before?
Why did he say that?
Would you be willing to swear that under oath?

1. _____
2. _____
3. _____
4. _____
5. _____

C

Picture Description

Describe the picture using the words below.

marriage vows	wedding ceremony
promising to love	wedding ring

_____
_____
_____
_____

✓ **Listen to the description of the picture.** ((Track 28))

A

Pronunciation Practice

In casual speech, you may hear the phrase "kind of" pronounced as "kinda."

Written	Spoken
1. I am kind of tired right now.	1. I'm kinda tired right now.
2. What kind of promise did you make to him?	2. What kinda promise did you make to him?
3. You won't believe the kind of bargains I got!	3. You won't believe the kinda bargains I got!

✓ **Now practice saying the following sentences.**

1. It is kind of sad how little people trust each other these days.
2. We only get the chance to see this kind of thing once every four years.
3. The oath they make is kind of long and complicated.

✓ **Now listen and repeat.** ((Track 29))

B

Conversation Pictures

Listen to the dialogs, and number the pictures. ((Track 30))

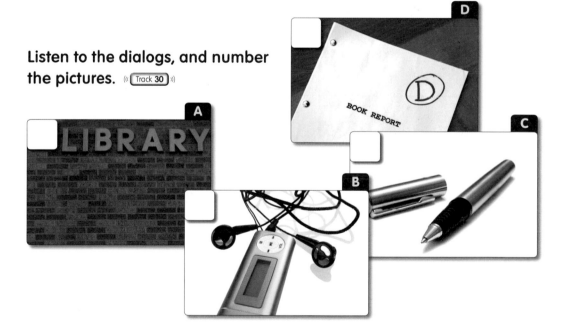

✓ **Now listen to the dialogs again, and choose the information related to the promise that is made.**

1. (A) after school   (B) end of class   (C) no friends   (D) not say anything
2. (A) after school   (B) end of class   (C) no friends   (D) not say anything
3. (A) after school   (B) end of class   (C) no friends   (D) not say anything
4. (A) after school   (B) end of class   (C) no friends   (D) not say anything

Short Dialogs

A

Dialog 1

Listen to the dialog and questions. Choose the best answer. ((Track 31))

1. (A) The man
   (C) Both the man and the woman
   (B) The woman
   (D) Neither the man nor the woman

2. (A) She can only share with him.
   (C) She gives the man her word.
   (B) She forgot.
   (D) She won't tell.

✓ **Listen again, and fill in the blanks.**

M: Do you have any ❶_____ what's wrong with Madison today? She sure seems upset about something.

W: Actually, I ❷_____ know. But I can't tell you.

M: What do you mean you ❸_____ tell me? I'm her friend, too. I want to know what's ❹_____.

W: Madison made me swear that I wouldn't ❺_____ anyone about it. That's why I can't tell you.

M: I'm sure she didn't ❻_____ that you couldn't tell me. You were just swearing not to tell ❼_____ people.

W: Sorry, Tom. A promise is a ❽_____. My lips are sealed.

B

Dialog 2

Listen to the dialog and questions. Choose the best answer. ((Track 32))

1. (A) He already left.
   (C) He has been late before.
   (B) He does not drink coffee.
   (D) He tried to call the woman.

2. (A) The man will leave a message for Sam.
   (B) The woman will leave for the office.
   (C) They will go somewhere else.
   (D) They will talk with Sam.

C

Dialog 3

Listen to the dialog, and write the names in the correct blanks. ((Track 33))

1. _____ has seen the raccoon.
2. _____ leaves food for the raccoon.
3. _____ wants to see the raccoon that night.
4. _____ suggests a window to watch from.

Joe

Sandra

Main Dialog

Listen to the dialog, and choose the best answer. ((Track 34))

1. What is the probable relationship of the speakers?
   - (A) Boss and co-worker
   - (B) Childhood friends
   - (C) Husband and wife
   - (D) Teacher and student

2. Which is true about the woman?
   - (A) She bought him a gift.
   - (B) She broke a promise.
   - (C) She lost her credit card.
   - (D) She works in a store.

3. What does the man suggest?
   - (A) Getting a new credit card
   - (B) Keeping her credit card
   - (C) Returning the items
   - (D) Swearing an oath

Listen again, and fill in the blanks. ((Track 35))

M: What in the world is this ❶_____ on our credit card for $120?

W: Oh. Didn't I mention to you that I bought some ❷_____ last weekend?

M: You did what? Joy, you swore that you wouldn't go on any more ❸_____ sprees until we got this credit card ❹_____.

W: I know, Mike. But they were having one of those going-out-of-business sales, and you would not believe the kind of ❺_____ I found!

M: I'm sure. It looks like you ❻_____ enough to spend over a hundred dollars that we really can't ❼_____ to spend!

W: I'm sorry, Mike. I ❽_____ I won't do anything like that again. I cross my heart.

M: You ❾_____ that before. I have a better idea this time. Give me your credit card, and I'll ❿_____ on to it until we get this bill completely paid off.

W: That could take ⓫_____!

M: Maybe. But if you keep going on these little shopping ⓬_____, we'll never get this credit card balance down to zero.

Short Talks

A
Short Talk 1

Listen to the short talk and questions. Choose the best answer. ((Track 36))

1. (A) His parents were the bride and groom.
   (B) It was not in a church.
   (C) The groom was twenty years old.
   (D) The people were already married.

2. (A) His best friend   (B) His parents
   (C) The couple's children   (D) The speaker

✓ **Listen again, and fill in the blanks.**

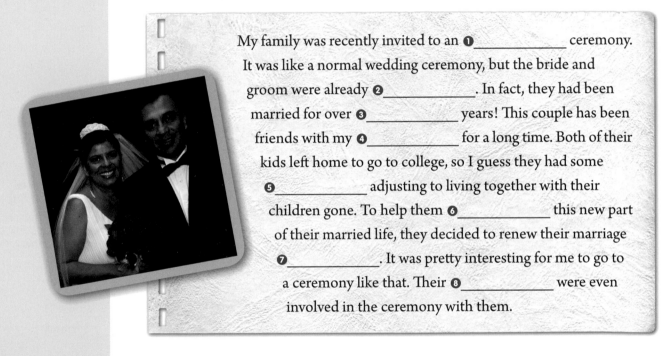

My family was recently invited to an ❶_____ ceremony. It was like a normal wedding ceremony, but the bride and groom were already ❷_____. In fact, they had been married for over ❸_____ years! This couple has been friends with my ❹_____ for a long time. Both of their kids left home to go to college, so I guess they had some ❺_____ adjusting to living together with their children gone. To help them ❻_____ this new part of their married life, they decided to renew their marriage ❼_____. It was pretty interesting for me to go to a ceremony like that. Their ❽_____ were even involved in the ceremony with them.

B
Short Talk 2

Listen to the short talk and questions. Choose the best answer. ((Track 37))

1. (A) A sworn oath in front of witnesses (B) A written and signed document
   (C) Someone's vow in a court of law   (D) Someone's word and a handshake

2. (A) A person shaking her hand   (B) A person signing in front of her
   (C) A person working with a lawyer   (D) A person writing down a promise

C
Short Talk 3

Listen to the short talk, and check (✓) the information that is true. ((Track 38))

- ☐ First time to see the ceremony
- ☐ No school
- ☐ Teacher will take an oath
- ☐ Happens every four years
- ☐ Practiced for four weeks
- ☐ Watch TV in class

Listen to the dialogs. Choose the correct picture. ((Track 39))

1. (A)   (B)   (C)

2. (A)   (B)   (C)

Listen to the dialogs and questions. Choose the best answer. ((Track 40))

3. (A) By email   (B) Chatting online
   (C) In person   (D) Over the phone

4. (A) At a bookstore   (B) In a cemetery
   (C) In her living room   (D) On the street

5. (A) Not to forget the plan   (B) To buy her a present
   (C) Not to look in the box   (D) To come to her birthday

6. (A) Moving   (B) Planning a party
   (C) Shopping   (D) Working in a restaurant

7. (A) Break the dishes   (B) Call another company
   (C) Use extra wrapping material   (D) Wash the dishes more carefully

8. (A) Classmates   (B) Co-workers
   (C) Siblings   (D) Strangers

9. (A) She broke her word.   (B) She gave her word to Steve.
   (C) She paid George some money.   (D) She vowed to give him a bonus.

Wrap-up

A Pre-listening Discussion

Talk about these questions.

1. What groups or organizations have special oaths?
2. Do you know any of these oaths? If so, can you say one?
3. Do you know anything about the famous Greek man Hippocrates?

B Listening Comprehension

Listen and answer the questions. Track 41

1. **When did Hippocrates live?**

____.

2. **What has one group written to replace the Hippocratic Oath?**

____.

3. **How many words are in the oath and in the charter?**

____.

C Dictation Practice

Listen again, and fill in the blanks. Track 42

The great ①________ doctor Hippocrates ②________ around 400 ③________. In addition ④____ healing people, ⑤____ also wrote ⑥________ the medical ⑦__________ of his ⑧________. Along with ⑨______ suggestions for ⑩______ doctors should ⑪________ about medicine, ⑫_____ described how ⑬____ believed doctors ⑭________ care for ⑮__________. In fact, ⑯________ of his ⑰________ became known ⑱____ the Hippocratic ⑲________ for doctors. ⑳________ the time ㉑____ Hippocrates, doctors ㉒________ promised to ㉓________ this oath. ㉔____ saying the ㉕________, doctors promise ㉖____ put a ㉗__________ health above ㉘______ else and ㉙____ respect the ㉚________ as a ㉛________.

The field ㉜____ medicine has ㉝________ many changes ㉞________ the days of Hippocrates. ㉟______ this reason, ㊱________ today believe ㊲______ Hippocratic Oath, ㊳________ its modern ㊴________, is out ㊵____ date by ㊶________ medical standards. ㊷__________, an international ㊸________ of doctors ㊹________ to write ㊺____ new kind ㊻____ oath better ㊼________ to medical ㊽______________ today. The ㊾________ that this ㊿________ created is (51)________ the Charter (52)____ Medical Professionalism. (53)________ the Hippocratic (54)________, it says (55)________ a patient's (56)________ should be (57)______ most important (58)________ for doctors. (59)____ also includes (60)________ to remind (61)________ that patients' (62)________ about treatment (63)________ to be (64)__________, even when (65)________ might (66)__________. Doctors (67)________ swear in (68)______ charter to (69)________ toward helping (70)______ poor get (71)________ medical care (72)________ need even (73)____ they can't (74)________ it.

Not (75)__________ wants to (76)________ to the (77)________ yet. Most (78)________ schools in (79)______ US still (80)________ doctors swear (81)____ version (82)____ the Hippocratic (83)________ upon graduation. (84)________ some schools (85)________ the charter (86)____ too long. (87)____ is almost (88)________ times longer (89)________ the Hippocratic (90)________. The original (91)________ by Hippocrates is about (92)________ words. The Charter (93)____ Medical Professionalism, (94)____ the other (95)________, is almost (96)________ words long!

Listening Test 🕘

PART I: Picture Description ((Track 43))

Listen and choose the statement that best describes what you see in the picture.

1.

(A) (B) (C) (D)

2.

(A) (B) (C) (D)

3.

(A) (B) (C) (D)

4.

(A)   (B)   (C)   (D)

5.

(A)   (B)   (C)   (D)

PART II: Questions and Responses ((Track 44))

Listen and choose the best response to each question.

6. (A)   (B)   (C)

7. (A)   (B)   (C)

8. (A)   (B)   (C)

9. (A)   (B)   (C)

10. (A)   (B)   (C)

PART III: Short Conversations ((Track 45))

You will hear two dialogs, each followed by three questions. Listen carefully, and choose the best answer to each question.

11. What is the woman going to do this weekend?
    - (A) Visit her mom and dad
    - (B) Clean his dirty clothes
    - (C) Make a promise to her brother
    - (D) Pick up her mom and dad

12. What does the man promise his sister?
    - (A) That he won't ask again
    - (B) That he'll be there Saturday morning
    - (C) That he won't bring his dirty clothes
    - (D) That he'll drive his car

13. When is the woman going to pick up her brother?
    - (A) When their parents arrive
    - (B) After she does her laundry
    - (C) Before the weekend
    - (D) Tomorrow morning

---

14. What is the man going to do?
    - (A) Take a final exam
    - (B) Make a reservation
    - (C) Meet some friends
    - (D) Help his friend study

15. When are the students probably going to meet?
    - (A) Friday afternoon
    - (B) As soon as the library opens
    - (C) After the next exam
    - (D) When he makes the reservation

16. What is the woman going to reserve?
    - (A) A book at the library
    - (B) A study room
    - (C) A computer
    - (D) A time to meet their professor

PART IV: Short Talks ((Track 46))

You will hear two talks, each followed by three questions. Listen carefully, and choose the best answer to each question.

17. What is going to happen on Wednesday?

    (A) They will buy some packing supplies.
    (B) The moving company is coming.
    (C) They are moving into a new building.
    (D) The boxes will be delivered to his house.

18. What does the speaker ask the staff to promise?

    (A) To call the moving company
    (B) To take his instructions seriously
    (C) To pack all their things
    (D) To arrive on time on Wednesday

19. What will happen if the people do not put their names on the boxes?

    (A) It'll be a disaster.
    (B) He'll check everything.
    (C) They'll need more packing supplies.
    (D) The truck will not leave.

---

20. What is the topic of the talk?

    (A) Why keeping a promise is important
    (B) Why people break their promises
    (C) Why you shouldn't break your promises
    (D) Why some people refuse to make promises

21. Why does the speaker think people break their promises?

    (A) Because it's easier to say yes than to say no
    (B) Because it's easy to make promises
    (C) Because everyone does it
    (D) Because people have many things to do

22. What advice does the speaker give about making your next promise?

    (A) To ask a friend or family member to help keep it
    (B) To take the easy way out
    (C) To ask yourself if it's a promise you can keep
    (D) To write down the promise so it seems more serious

Special Occasions

Warm-up

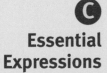

A

Look & Listen

Listen to the dialogs. Write the number next to the speakers. ((Track 47))

B

Listen Again

Listen again, and match the occasion with the item mentioned by the speakers. ((Track 48))

1. Birthday •
2. Baby Shower •
3. Anniversary •
4. Graduation •

• (A) Chess set
• (B) Gift card
• (C) Gift certificate
• (D) Watch

C

Essential Expressions

Put the words and phrases into the right categories.

fundraising event	invitation	baby shower	cap and gown
belated birthday gift	gift certificate	decorations	toast
	graduation ceremony	wedding anniversary	

Occasions	Things
_____	_____
_____	_____
_____	_____
_____	_____
_____	_____
_____	_____

Listening Practice

Listen. Write the answer. ((Track 49))

> A few friends came, but it was mainly family. I don't remember.
>
> Not as many as I thought it would win. Yes, that's correct.
>
> I don't think anyone has planned one for her yet.

1. _____

2. _____

3. _____

4. _____

5. _____

Listen. Write the question. ((Track 50))

> Where will the graduation ceremony be held?
>
> Did you watch the Fourth of July fireworks?
>
> Did your company's fundraising event go well?
>
> When is Thanksgiving in your country?
>
> What are you going to do with those red envelopes?

1. _____

2. _____

3. _____

4. _____

5. _____

Describe the picture using the words below.

candles	wrapped
decorations	cake

_____

_____

_____

_____

✓ **Listen to the description of the picture.** ((Track 51))

Speaking Practice

A

Intonation Practice

In certain four-syllable statements or questions, the stress will usually be on the last syllable. Study the following statements and questions that typically have the stress pattern "dum dum dum da."

Written	Spoken
1. It is really good.	1. It's really **good**.
2. How did you do?	2. How did you **do?**
3. We will see you then.	3. We'll see you **then**.

✓ **Now practice saying the following sentences. Remember to stress the last syllable.**

1. It's so much fun!
2. When is she due?
3. I've got one, too.

✓ **Now listen and repeat.** ((Track 52))

B

Conversation Pictures

Listen to the dialogs, and number the pictures. ((Track 53))

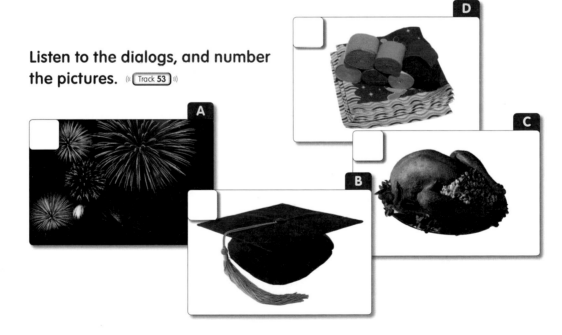

✓ **Now listen to the dialogs again, and choose the thing mentioned by the speakers.**

1. (A) crowds   (B) decorations   (C) invitation   (D) photos
2. (A) crowds   (B) decorations   (C) invitation   (D) photos
3. (A) crowds   (B) decorations   (C) invitation   (D) photos
4. (A) crowds   (B) decorations   (C) invitation   (D) photos

Short Dialogs

A

Dialog 1

Listen to the dialog and questions. Choose the best answer. ((Track 54))

1. (A) China   (B) England
   (C) Japan   (D) Mexico

2. (A) Children   (B) Dessert
   (C) Luck   (D) The moon

✓ **Listen again, and fill in the blanks.**

W: I have to ❶_____ at the supermarket on North Street to pick up a ❷_____ of mandarin oranges that my mother ordered for ❸_____ New Year.

M: Why do you need so many ❹_____?

W: The mandarin orange is a symbol of good ❺_____ and prosperity for the Chinese. Celebrating by decorating the ❻_____ with oranges is an important tradition in my family. We ❼_____ them as well.

M: Chinese New Year sounds ❽_____.

B

Dialog 2

Listen to the dialog and questions. Choose the best answer. ((Track 55))

1. (A) Family   (B) Friends
   (C) Both speakers   (D) Both friends and family

2. (A) The number of grandchildren   (B) The number of guests at the party
   (C) The number of years of marriage   (D) The person's age

C

Dialog 3

Listen to the dialog, and complete each statement. ((Track 56))

1. The speakers are talking about a company's _____.

2. The man was surprised because the event _____
   _____.

Main Dialog

Listen to the dialog, and choose the best answer. ((Track 57))

1. How long has Paul been a new father?
   - (A) One day
   - (B) Several days
   - (C) A few weeks
   - (D) Over a month

2. Who is helping them out at home?
   - (A) His wife's aunt
   - (B) His wife's mother
   - (C) His wife's parents
   - (D) His wife's sister

3. Who is his daughter named after?
   - (A) His favorite flower
   - (B) His grandmother
   - (C) His mother
   - (D) His wife

Listen again, and fill in the blanks. ((Track 58))

W: Congratulations, Paul! I heard that your twins were born last ❶_____! How does it feel to be a new father?

M: It feels wonderful! Of course, I haven't had more than three or four hours of sleep in ❷_____, but everyone tells me that this is ❸_____.

W: You'll be lucky if you get any rest at all in the next few ❹_____!

M: As if I didn't know.

W: How about your ❺_____? How is she doing? I can't imagine ❻_____ birth to twins.

M: She's doing really well. Her ❼_____ is staying with us right now, so that's a big ❽_____ for both of us.
Oh, I brought a few pictures of the twins with me to the ❾_____ today. Here, have a look.

W: They are adorable! So, have you and your wife ❿_____ on names yet?

M: Yes, we're going to name our baby girl Rose after my ⓫_____, and our baby boy will be William after Carla's ⓬ _____.

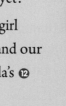

Short Talks

Listen to the short talk and questions. Choose the best answer. (((Track 59)))

1. (A) The bride's brother
   (C) The groom
   (B) The bride's father
   (D) The groom's friend

2. (A) On the night they buy their rings
   (C) During the wedding ceremony
   (B) Before the wedding ceremony
   (D) At a party after the marriage ceremony

✓ **Listen again, and fill in the blanks.**

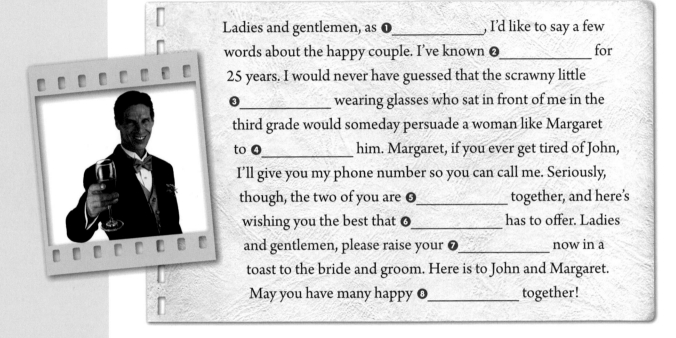

Ladies and gentlemen, as ❶_____, I'd like to say a few words about the happy couple. I've known ❷_____ for 25 years. I would never have guessed that the scrawny little ❸_____ wearing glasses who sat in front of me in the third grade would someday persuade a woman like Margaret to ❹_____ him. Margaret, if you ever get tired of John, I'll give you my phone number so you can call me. Seriously, though, the two of you are ❺_____ together, and here's wishing you the best that ❻_____ has to offer. Ladies and gentlemen, please raise your ❼_____ now in a toast to the bride and groom. Here is to John and Margaret. May you have many happy ❽_____ together!

Listen to the short talk and questions. Choose the best answer. (((Track 60)))

1. (A) Chen
   (C) Lennon
   (B) Dolittle
   (D) Lopez

2. (A) Chen
   (C) Lennon
   (B) Dolittle
   (D) Lopez

Listen to the short talk, and complete the note diagrams. (((Track 61)))

The first Thanksgiving	A typical Thanksgiving
• celebrated by _____ settlers in _____ • celebrated _____ and _____	• roast _____ with _____ and gravy, sweet _____, and _____ pie for dessert

Listening Quiz

 05:21

Listen to the dialogs. Choose the correct picture. ((Track 62))

A

HAPPY ANNIVERSARY

B

Baby Shower

C

1. (A)   (B)   (C)

2. (A)   (B)   (C)

Listen to the dialogs and questions. Choose the best answer. ((Track 63))

3. (A) A business's tenth anniversary   (B) A child's tenth birthday
   (C) Ten years of marriage   (D) Valentine's Day

4. (A) Earned his high school diploma   (B) Finished university
   (C) Had his school picture taken   (D) Passed his entrance exam

5. (A) He arrived late for the party.   (B) He bought a gift for her.
   (C) He celebrated his birthday.   (D) He sent her flowers.

6. (A) The man   (B) The woman
   (C) Both the man and the woman   (D) Neither the man nor the woman

7. (A) Singing   (B) Costumes
   (C) Fireworks   (D) Lights

8. (A) Bride and groom   (B) Classmates
   (C) Co-workers   (D) Strangers

9. (A) All of the employees   (B) The future of the company
   (C) The new larger office space   (D) Their happy life together

A

Pre-listening Discussion

Talk about these questions.

1. What is a reasonable amount to spend on a child's birthday present?
2. Do guests usually receive something from the host at parties in your country?
3. How much might parents in your country spend on a child's birthday party?

B

Listening Comprehension

Listen and answer the questions. ((Track 64))

1. **What kinds of things were usually put inside the first goody bags?**

   _____.

2. **How much do goody bags usually cost these days?**

   _____.

3. **What is a suggested alternative for parents who don't want to give out goody bags?**

   _____.

C

Dictation Practice

Listen again, and fill in the blanks. ((Track 65))

Have you ❶_____ been to ❷____ party where ❸_____ guests got ❹_____ expensive gifts ❺_____ the person ❻____ honor at ❼_____ party? That ❽_____ sound strange, ❾_____ it has ❿_____ happened at ⓫_____ children's birthday ⓬_____ in the ⓭____ . That is ⓮_____ the tradition ⓯____ giving guests ⓰_____ bags at ⓱_____ end of ⓲_____ party has ⓳_____ out of ⓴_____ .

It is ㉑_____ to say ㉒_____ when and ㉓_____ the tradition ㉔____ giving goody ㉕_____ at birthday ㉖_____ began. At ㉗_____ since the ㉘_____ , parents hosting ㉙_____ parties have ㉚_____ giving out ㉛_____ gift bags. ㉜_____ early bags ㉝_____ typically simple ㉞_____ cheap. Each ㉟_____ who came ㊱____ the party ㊲_____ receive a ㊳_____ bag with ㊴_____ candy and ㊵_____ a few ㊶_____ in it ㊷____ they left. ㊸_____ , somewhere along ㊹_____ line, a ㊺_____ between parents ㊻_____ . The parents ㊼____ the next ㊽_____ boy or ㊾_____ would try ㊿____ create a 51_____ gift bag 52_____ their party 53_____ . They might 54_____ for nicer 55_____ , put in 56_____ candy, or 57_____ out better 58_____ . Then came 59_____ idea of 60_____ small toys 61____ goody bags. 62_____ there, things 63_____ snowballed into 64_____ situation we 65_____ today. Whereas 66_____ first goody 67_____ cost well 68_____ a dollar 69_____ , goody bags 70_____ usually cost 71_____ between three 72____ five dollars 73_____ . Goody bags 74____ fancy theme 75_____ can even 76_____ host parents 77____ to twenty 78_____ per bag!

79_____ parents these 80_____ are looking 81_____ a way 82_____ of all 83_____ goody bag 84_____ . They like 85_____ idea of 86_____ guests a 87_____ gift to 88_____ home to 89_____ the party, 90_____ . One alternative 91____ goody bags 92____ to have 93_____ make their 94_____ gift to 95_____ home. It 96_____ be a 97_____ picture frame 98_____ a picture 99_____ the party 100____ a handmade 101_____ . Any kind 102____ small kids' 103_____ works, as 104_____ as it's 105_____ and easy 106____ make.

Listening Test

PART I: Picture Description ((Track 66))

Listen and choose the statement that best describes what you see in the picture.

1.

(A)   (B)   (C)   (D)

2.

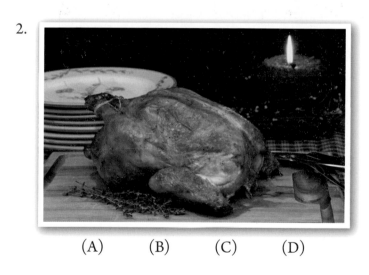

(A)   (B)   (C)   (D)

3.

(A)   (B)   (C)   (D)

4.

(A) (B) (C) (D)

5.

(A) (B) (C) (D)

PART II: Questions and Responses ((Track 67))

Listen and choose the best response to each question.

6. (A) (B) (C)

7. (A) (B) (C)

8. (A) (B) (C)

9. (A) (B) (C)

10. (A) (B) (C)

PART III: Short Conversations ((Track 68))

You will hear two dialogs, each followed by three questions. Listen carefully, and choose the best answer to each question.

11. Why didn't the man go to the party?

    (A) He was with his family.
    (B) He had to work.
    (C) He was taking photos.
    (D) He was not invited.

12. What kind of party was it?

    (A) A costume party
    (B) An anniversary celebration
    (C) An adult's birthday party
    (D) A child's birthday party

13. What made the party interesting?

    (A) A performer
    (B) The games
    (C) Special food
    (D) The music

---

14. Which is true about the woman in the conversation?

    (A) She is related to Scott.
    (B) She is 15 years older than the couple.
    (C) She was there when the couple met.
    (D) She has not known the couple very long.

15. What were the women doing when the man walked up?

    (A) Talking at a table
    (B) Dancing together
    (C) Eating their dinner
    (D) Looking for a friend

16. What did Scott ask Susan to do the night they met?

    (A) To talk to a friend
    (B) To marry him
    (C) To go to a movie
    (D) To dance with him

PART IV: Short Talks ((Track 69))

You will hear two talks, each followed by three questions. Listen carefully, and choose the best answer to each question.

17. What was shocking about the bride's dress?

    (A) It was too short.
    (B) It was extremely expensive.
    (C) It had feathers.
    (D) It was very old.

18. How did the people react?

    (A) They took pictures.
    (B) They laughed.
    (C) They smiled but kept quiet.
    (D) They left early.

19. What does the speaker imply about the reception?

    (A) It was held at a different location.
    (B) It was also shocking.
    (C) It was like her own reception.
    (D) It was longer than the wedding.

___

20. What successful event did the chapter plan and host?

    (A) A graduation
    (B) An award ceremony
    (C) A state conference
    (D) A reading group

21. What did the feedback say about the state conference?

    (A) They had a lot of attendees this year.
    (B) Last year's conference was better.
    (C) It was significantly better than last year's.
    (D) Not enough helpers from the chapter joined them.

22. What was the exciting news?

    (A) They raised $20,000.
    (B) They had an outstanding year.
    (C) The conference was in the news.
    (D) A famous person stood up.

Steps and Plans

Warm-up

A

Look & Listen

Listen to the dialogs. Write the number next to the speakers. ((Track 70))

B

Listen Again

Listen again, and fill in the blanks. ((Track 71))

1. The woman doesn't know how to _____.
2. The woman doesn't know how to _____.
3. The man doesn't know how to _____.
4. The man doesn't know how to _____.

C

Essential Expressions

Circle the best word or phrase to complete each sentence.

1. (After / When) you are doing that, be sure not to get the cloth wet.
2. The (last / next) step is to click "finish" in the pop-up window.
3. (Before / Once) you have cut the picture to the right size, put it in the frame.
4. (In addition to / To begin with), he has to clean the table and wash the dishes.
5. The presentation will be (followed by / then) a 15-minute break for coffee and snacks.
6. In (addition to / the first) that, be sure there is no extra glue around the edges.
7. Mixing all of the wet ingredients in the bowl is the (final / next) thing to do.
8. Select the print option from the tool bar as the first (place / step) of the process.
9. The sauce is ready to use, but (after / until) then, keep it in the refrigerator.
10. (First of all / Ultimately), she chose her pattern before she drew it on the paper.

Listening Practice

A

How would you answer?

Listen. Write the answer. ((Track 72))

> Then they should clean up.
> Next, he has to select which options he wants.
> Nothing. That's all you need to do.
> Sure, let's think of some ideas together.
> I'm afraid not, because of your dentist appointment.

1. _____
2. _____
3. _____
4. _____
5. _____

B

How would you ask?

Listen. Write the question. ((Track 73))

> What does she have to do? How did you make it?
> What's your schedule like on Tuesday? That's it, right?
> Can you teach me how to work this thing?

1. _____
2. _____
3. _____
4. _____
5. _____

C

Picture Description

Describe the picture using the words below.

added	crossed out
indicates	scheduled for

_____

_____

_____

✓ **Listen to the description of the picture.** ((Track 74))

Speaking Practice

A

Pronunciation Practice

In casual speech, you may hear the phrase "ought to" pronounced as "oughta."

Written	Spoken
1. The lesson ought to be over by 4:30. 2. You ought to update that program. 3. This box ought to be big enough.	1. The lesson oughta be over by 4:30. 2. You oughta update that program. 3. This box oughta be big enough.

✓ **Now practice saying the following sentences.**

1. Then it ought to work.
2. Everybody ought to read it.
3. The class ought to be required for all students.

✓ **Now listen and repeat.** ((Track 75))

B

Conversation Pictures

Listen to the dialogs, and number the pictures. ((Track 76))

✓ **Now listen to the dialogs again, and choose the time mentioned by the speakers.**

1. (A) Past   (B) Present   (C) Future
2. (A) Past   (B) Present   (C) Future
3. (A) Past   (B) Present   (C) Future
4. (A) Past   (B) Present   (C) Future

Short Dialogs

Listen to the dialog and questions. Choose the best answer. (((Track 77)))

1. (A) Mondays   (B) Wednesdays
   (C) Fridays   (D) Weekends

2. (A) Completing homework   (B) Eating dinner
   (C) Exercising   (D) Practicing an instrument

✓ **Listen again, and fill in the blanks.**

G1: What's the ❶_____ day of the week for you?

G2: ❷_____. I've got classes at school, then
❸_____ practice at four p.m., followed by
❹_____ lessons.

G1: Wow! That's a really ❺_____ day! When do you
have time to do your ❻_____?

G2: I get home around 7:30, so there is still ❼_____
of time to do homework after I get home and have
❽_____.

Listen to the dialog and questions. Choose the best answer. (((Track 78)))

1. (A) Be sure you have a lot of free time.   (B) Follow the directions carefully.
   (C) Get good ingredients.   (D) Use the right equipment.

2. (A) He enjoys baking.   (B) He needs a better oven.
   (C) He took lessons from the woman.   (D) He works in a restaurant.

Listen to the dialog, and put the steps in order. (((Track 79)))

_____ (A) Close

_____ (B) Load

_____ (C) Pour

_____ (D) Select

Main Dialog

A

Listen

Listen to the dialog, and choose the best answer. ((Track 80))

1. Which of the following art supplies were NOT mentioned by the speakers?
   - (A) Cloth
   - (B) Dyes
   - (C) String
   - (D) Wax

2. What was the first color used by the man?
   - (A) Blue
   - (B) Green
   - (C) White
   - (D) Yellow

3. How long did he work on the scarf?
   - (A) A few hours
   - (B) Overnight
   - (C) A number of days
   - (D) Over one week

B

Listen Again

Listen again, and fill in the blanks. ((Track 81))

W: Wow, how did you make this beautiful
   ❶_____?

M: It was quite easy. After deciding on a
   ❷_____, I chose three different
   colors to dye the cloth with.

W: I can see that you chose green,
   ❸_____, and yellow. But how did you prevent the
   ❹_____ dye from getting to the parts where you
   ❺_____ blue or yellow?

M: I used wax to seal those ❻_____ of the scarf off from the dye.
   That way, when you dip the ❼_____ into the green dye, only
   some parts absorb the dye.

W: Let me guess. After that, you ❽_____ the wax from the other
   parts, cover the green parts with ❾_____, and then dip the cloth
   in blue or yellow dye!

M: That's right! But you have to let the cloth ❿_____ first, or the
   pattern won't look as nice when you finish.

W: It must have taken a long time for you to ⓫_____ the whole
   thing.

M: It took me about ⓬_____ days, just because I had to let the
   fabric dry overnight before I could do the next color.

Short Talks

Short Talk 1

Listen to the short talk and questions. Choose the best answer. ((Track 82))

1. (A) A microwave   (B) Boiling water
   (C) Hot oil   (D) The oven

2. (A) Chilies   (B) Eggs
   (C) Garlic   (D) Prawns

✓ **Listen again, and fill in the blanks.**

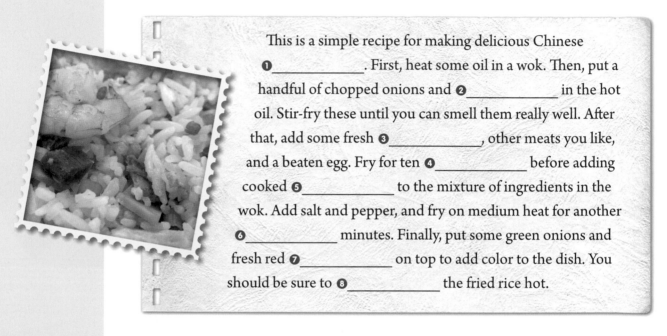

This is a simple recipe for making delicious Chinese ❶_____. First, heat some oil in a wok. Then, put a handful of chopped onions and ❷_____ in the hot oil. Stir-fry these until you can smell them really well. After that, add some fresh ❸_____, other meats you like, and a beaten egg. Fry for ten ❹_____ before adding cooked ❺_____ to the mixture of ingredients in the wok. Add salt and pepper, and fry on medium heat for another ❻_____ minutes. Finally, put some green onions and fresh red ❼_____ on top to add color to the dish. You should be sure to ❽_____ the fried rice hot.

B

Short Talk 2

Listen to the short talk and questions. Choose the best answer. ((Track 83))

1. (A) Children   (B) Clients
   (C) Employees   (D) Siblings

2. (A) To increase production speed   (B) To make more money through sales
   (C) To reduce work errors   (D) To use less of something

C

Short Talk 3

Listen to the short talk, and match the information that goes together. ((Track 8

1. Arranged guides   •   • (A) Friends
2. Recommended an agency   •   • (B) Brother
3. Traveled together   •   • (C) Agent

A

Picture Matching

Listen to the dialogs. Choose the correct picture. ((Track 85))

1. (A)   (B)   (C)

2. (A)   (B)   (C)

B

Listen & Choose

Listen to the dialogs and questions. Choose the best answer. ((Track 86))

3. (A) Bowling   (B) Cleaning
   (C) Helping his mother   (D) Studying

4. (A) How to cut them   (B) How to fertilize them
   (C) How to plant them   (D) How to water them

5. (A) Look at flights   (B) Look at hotels
   (C) Look at their money   (D) Look at their weekend schedule

6. (A) School   (B) Soccer
   (C) Studying   (D) Swimming

7. (A) Fun, studying, sports, school   (B) School, sports, studying, fun
   (C) Sports, fun, school, studying   (D) Studying, school, fun, sports

8. (A) Lawyer   (B) Manager
   (C) Sports coach   (D) Teacher

9. (A) Assigning for or against   (B) Learning to organize
   (C) Making groups   (D) Switching sides

A

Pre-listening
Discussion

B

Listening
Comprehension

C

Dictation
Practice

Talk about these questions.

1. How many potted plants do you have at home?
2. What does a person need to do to take care of potted plants?
3. Do you know how to change a plant's pot? If so, what are the steps?

Listen and answer the questions. ((Track 87))

1. **What is the first step suggested by the speaker?**

_____.

2. **When a plant won't easily come out of its pot, what can you use to get the job done?**

_____.

3. **What should you do with a plant after it is in its new pot?**

_____.

Listen again, and fill in the blanks. ((Track 88))

If you ❶_____ like me, ❷_____ probably have ❸____ couple of ❹_____ plants around ❺_____ apartment or ❻_____. Have those ❼_____ been in ❽_____ same old ❾_____ for a ❿_____ time? If ⓫____, then it ⓬_____ be time ⓭____ put them ⓮_____ new pots. ⓯_____ a plant ⓰____ a new ⓱_____ isn't difficult. ⓲_____ just need ⓳____ keep in ⓴_____ a few ㉑_____ tips so ㉒_____ your plant ㉓_____ get the ㉔_____ benefit from ㉕_____ move.

Before ㉖_____ actually try ㉗____ move a ㉘_____ from an ㉙_____ pot to ㉚____ new one, ㉛_____ should water ㉜_____ plant really ㉝_____ and let ㉞____ sit for ㉟____ day or ㊱_____. It will ㊲____ easier to ㊳_____ with the ㊴_____ if the ㊵_____ is a ㊶_____ wet.

When ㊷_____ are ready ㊸____ take the ㊹_____ out of ㊺____ old pot, ㊻_____ by carefully ㊼_____ your hand ㊽_____ over the ㊾_____ of the ㊿_____ pot. The ⓼_____ of the ⓽_____ should be ⓾_____ two of ⓾_____ fingers. Then ㊋_____ the pot ㊌_____ down and ㊍_____ the edge ㊎____ the pot ㊏____ something. If ㊐_____ plant does ㊑_____ easily come ㊒_____ of the ㊓_____ by doing ㊔_____, try tapping ㊕_____. You can ㊖_____ the tapping ㊗____ using a ㊘_____ to loosen ㊙_____ soil around ㊚_____ inside of ㊛_____ pot. The ㊜_____ should come ㊝_____ after that.

㊞_____ you have ㊟_____ plant out ㊠____ its old ㊡_____, you are ㊢_____ to move ㊣____ to its ㊤_____ home. There ㊥_____ be enough ㊦_____ in the ㊧_____ of the ㊨_____ pot so ㊩_____ the plant ㊪_____ about three ㊫_____ below the ㊬_____ of the ㊭_____. Pour dirt ㊮_____ the new ㊯_____ all around ㊰_____ roots and ㊱_____ the soil ㊲_____ lightly. After ㊳_____, give the ㊴_____ some water ㊵_____ keep it ㊶_____ of direct ㊷_____ for about ㊸_____ week. That ㊹____ all it ㊺_____ to move ㊻____ plant to ㊼____ new pot!

Listening Test 🕘 09:22

PART I: Picture Description (((Track 89)))

Listen and choose the statement that best describes what you see in the picture.

1.

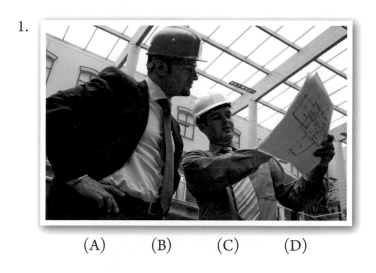

(A)   (B)   (C)   (D)

2.

(A)   (B)   (C)   (D)

3.

(A)   (B)   (C)   (D)

4.

    (A)   (B)   (C)   (D)

5.

    (A)   (B)   (C)   (D)

PART II: Questions and Responses (((Track 90)))

Listen and choose the best response to each question.

6. (A)   (B)   (C)

7. (A)   (B)   (C)

8. (A)   (B)   (C)

9. (A)   (B)   (C)

10. (A)   (B)   (C)

PART III: Short Conversations ((Track 91))

You will hear two dialogs, each followed by three questions. Listen carefully, and choose the best answer to each question.

11. What does the woman ask the man?

   (A) What time the trolley bus arrives
   (B) Where the courthouse is
   (C) If he rides the trolley bus
   (D) Where the trolley bus goes

12. What is the trolley's second stop?

   (A) The bus stop
   (B) The courthouse
   (C) The university
   (D) Market Square

13. Where does the woman want to go?

   (A) The bus stop
   (B) The courthouse
   (C) The university
   (D) Market Square

---

14. How did the woman describe her date?

   (A) It was exhausting.
   (B) It was fancy.
   (C) It was perfect.
   (D) It was boring.

15. Where did the woman's date start?

   (A) At the movies
   (B) At a restaurant
   (C) At the dance club
   (D) At her apartment

16. How did she feel by the end of the night?

   (A) She was exhausted.
   (B) She was excited.
   (C) She was sad.
   (D) She was relaxed.

PART IV: Short Talks ((Track 92))

You will hear two talks, each followed by three questions. Listen carefully, and choose the best answer to each question.

17. When does the class have their first presentation?

  (A) Next week
  (B) This week
  (C) The next day
  (D) Next month

18. Why is it important to stay within the time limit?

  (A) Because there are a lot of steps
  (B) Because he doesn't want them to read
  (C) Because they have a big class
  (D) Because it makes them practice more

19. What is the final step?

  (A) To create an outline
  (B) To take a few deep breaths
  (C) To choose a good topic
  (D) To review the topic with the class

---

20. What time does the speaker's first class start?

  (A) 8:00
  (B) 9:00
  (C) 10:30
  (D) She doesn't say.

21. What does the speaker do during her two-hour break?

  (A) Meet her friends for lunch
  (B) Run across campus
  (C) Study in the cafeteria
  (D) Work in the library

22. What's the best thing about her schedule?

  (A) She doesn't have to run across campus.
  (B) Her first and second classes are in the same building.
  (C) She never gets stuck in rush-hour traffic.
  (D) She goes to school two days a week.

UNIT 5 Music

A
Look & Listen

B
Listen Again

C
Essential Expressions

Warm-up

Listen to the dialogs. Write the number next to the speakers. ((Track 93))

Listen again, and write the kinds of music the speakers mention. ((Track 94))

The men like:

_____

_____

The women like:

_____

_____

Write the missing words to make correct expressions.

| balcony | evening | fast | first | professional |
| repetitive | soothing | stage | street | traditional |

1. _____ beat – a quick tempo
2. _____ chair – the place where the best musician for a given instrument sits
3. _____ fright – a feeling of fear about performing in front of people
4. _____ music – music that has a long history of importance
5. _____ musician – a person who plays music on sidewalks, corners, etc.
6. _____ performance – a show that begins after 5:00 p.m.
7. _____ rhythm – a rhythm that sounds the same over and over
8. _____ seats – an area for seating above the main floor of a theater
9. _____ singer – a person who sings as his or her job
10. _____ song – a song that is relaxing

Listening Practice

Listen. Write the answer. ((Track 95))

> It sounds a bit like polka music.   It's called folk music.
> I don't know. I've never heard them before.   Not yet. Is it any good?
> I've heard it before, but I can't think of the name.

1. _____
2. _____
3. _____
4. _____
5. _____

Listen. Write the question. ((Track 96))

> Could you turn up the radio?   Have you taken lessons before?
> Do you often go to classical concerts?   What instrument do you play?
> Are you going to the music festival this weekend?

1. _____
2. _____
3. _____
4. _____
5. _____

Describe the picture using the words below.

| dancing | holding |
| listening | playing |

_____
_____
_____
_____

✓ **Listen to the description of the picture.** ((Track 97))

Speaking Practice

A

Intonation Practice

In certain four-syllable statements or questions, the stress will usually be on the first and third syllables. Study the following statements and questions that typically have the stress pattern "da dum da dum."

Written	Spoken
1. I don't like it.	1. **I** don't **like** it.
2. He is dancing.	2. **He** is **danc**ing
3. You look tired.	3. **You** look **tired.**

✓ **Now practice saying the following sentences. Remember to stress the first and third syllables.**

1. She drinks coffee.
2. Loud is better.
3. That's my trumpet.

✓ **Now listen and repeat.** ((Track 98))

B

Conversation Pictures

Listen to the dialogs, and number the pictures. ((Track 99))

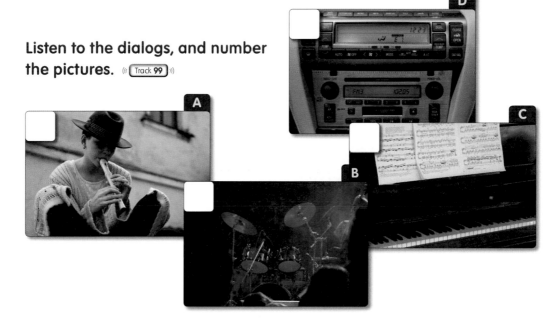

✓ **Now listen to the dialogs again, and choose the thing mentioned by the speakers.**

1. (A) Fun   (B) Incredible   (C) Lovely   (D) Soothing
2. (A) Fun   (B) Incredible   (C) Lovely   (D) Soothing
3. (A) Fun   (B) Incredible   (C) Lovely   (D) Soothing
4. (A) Fun   (B) Incredible   (C) Lovely   (D) Soothing

Short Dialogs

Dialog 1

Listen to the dialog and questions. Choose the best answer. ((Track 100))

1. (A) He can play the song.   (B) He doesn't like the song.
   (C) He gave her the music box.   (D) He recognizes the song.

2. (A) The woman   (B) The woman's mother
   (C) The woman's grandmother   (D) The woman's son

✓ **Listen again, and fill in the blanks.**

M: Where is that ❶_____ coming from?

W: Oh, that's from my ❷_____ over on the mantel.

M: It sounds very ❸_____. What song is it?

W: It's Brahms' ❹_____. I would listen to it every night as a ❺_____.

M: So, you've had the music box for a ❻_____ time?

W: Yes, my ❼_____ gave to my ❽_____, who gave it to me.

B

Dialog 2

Listen to the dialog and questions. Choose the best answer. ((Track 101))

1. (A) Its price   (B) Its simplicity
   (C) Its usefulness   (D) Its weight

2. (A) Its popularity   (B) Its simplicity
   (C) Its versatility   (D) Its size

C

Dialog 3

Listen to the dialog, and write the correct information. ((Track 102))

1. Music they will hear: _____

2. Performers: city _____ and professional _____

Main Dialog

Listen to the dialog, and choose the best answer. ((Track 103))

1. What kinds of musical instruments were played at the concert?
   - (A) Drums
   - (B) Guitars
   - (C) Violins
   - (D) None

2. Where does the woman think they can get tickets?
   - (A) From her friend
   - (B) From the box office
   - (C) From the Internet
   - (D) From the performers

3. When do they hope to see the performance?
   - (A) Saturday afternoon
   - (B) Saturday night
   - (C) Sunday afternoon
   - (D) Sunday night

Listen again, and fill in the blanks. ((Track 104))

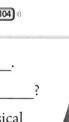

W: I went to a concert last ❶_____.

M: What was the music being ❷_____?

W: All different kinds, but no one used musical ❸_____.

M: How was that possible?

W: They used trash can ❹_____, brooms, and even their feet to stomp on the stage.

M: That sounds ❺_____. I'd love to have seen that.

W: I wouldn't mind seeing the performance ❻_____. Maybe we can find cheap tickets if we go to the ❼_____ next weekend right before the performance.

M: Do you think someone might be ❽_____ tickets in front of the theater?

W: No, but sometimes people ❾_____ tickets and then can't come to the show for one ❿_____ or another. In that case, the box office might sell us the tickets at a discounted price.

M: I guess it wouldn't hurt to try. What time is the performance on ⓫_____?

W: There is an early evening performance that day. It starts at ⓬_____ p.m.

Short Talks

Listen to the short talk and questions. Choose the best answer. ((Track 105))

1. (A) A kind of drum
   (C) A wind instrument
   (B) A string instrument
   (D) An electronic instrument

2. (A) She asked him to play it again.
   (C) She introduced him to her mother.
   (B) She gave him money.
   (D) She sang along with him.

✓ **Listen again, and fill in the blanks.**

On my way home from the ❶_____ yesterday, I heard a man playing the ❷_____ in the subway station. He was playing an old ❸_____ song, but he wasn't singing of course. I recognized the song because it is one of my ❹_____ favorites. She has an album with that ❺_____ on it, and she plays it a lot while she does ❻_____. I guess the song reminded me of my mother because while I listened, it really lifted my spirits. I had to throw a few ❼_____ into the man's hat when he was finished. I don't ❽_____ do that, but this time I made an exception.

Listen to the short talk and questions. Choose the best answer. ((Track 106))

1. (A) Conductor
   (C) Musician
   (B) Music teacher
   (D) Violin maker

2. (A) She plays the violin.
   (C) She works at a music school.
   (B) She taught Sandra to play.
   (D) She writes her own music.

Listen to the short talk, and write T for true or F for false for each statement. ((Track 107))

1. _____ The speaker implies that many people usually attend the festival.
2. _____ Jasmine declines the invitation to go to the festival.

A

Picture Matching

Listen to the dialogs. Choose the correct picture. ((Track 108))

 **A**

 **B**

 **C**

1. (A)   (B)   (C)

2. (A)   (B)   (C)

B

Listen & Choose

Listen to the dialogs and questions. Choose the best answer. ((Track 109))

3. (A) In a dance club   (B) In a music store
   (C) In a theater   (D) In a car

4. (A) Listening to a jazz band (B) Performing in a festival
   (C) Shopping in a downtown store (D) Studying Beethoven

5. (A) Instrumental music   (B) Opera music
   (C) Pop music   (D) Vocal music

6. (A) Disgusted   (B) Annoyed
   (C) Bored   (D) Surprised

7. (A) The drummer   (B) The guitarist
   (C) The man   (D) The singer

8. (A) They heard recorded music. (B) They perform music together.
   (C) They went to school together. (D) They will graduate soon.

9. (A) At a concert   (B) At a dance
   (C) In band class   (D) In elevators

Wrap-up

A Pre-listening Discussion

Talk about these questions.

1. What is a famous song from a movie? What movie is it from?
2. Can you sing or play any theme songs from movies?
3. What movie has a great soundtrack?

B Listening Comprehension

Listen and answer the questions. (Track 110)

1. **How does music in movies help audiences?**

   ______________________________.

2. **Which song from the *Wizard of Oz* does the speaker mention?**

   ______________________________.

3. **From which two movies do the speaker's favorite theme songs come?**

   ______________________________.

C Dictation Practice

Listen again, and fill in the blanks. (Track 111)

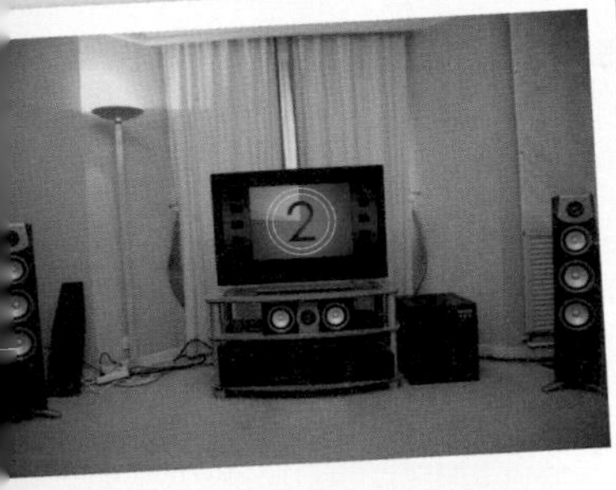

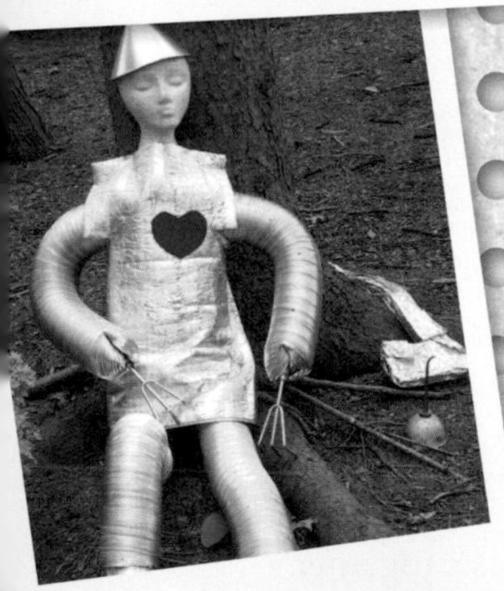

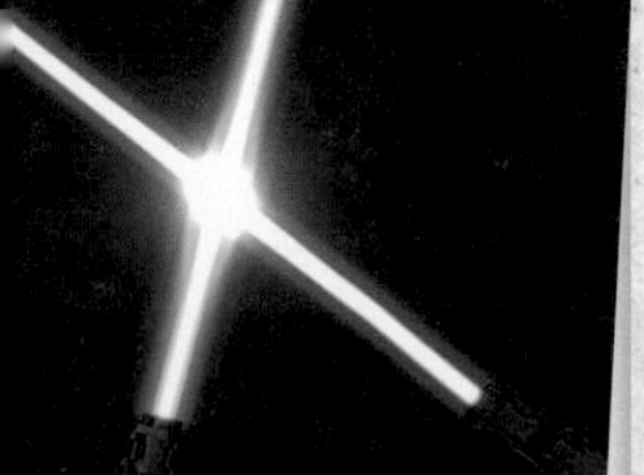

Even from ① ____ early days ② ____ movie making, ③ ____ played an ④ ____ part in ⑤ ____ stories on ⑥ ____. The right ⑦ ____ or music ⑧ ____ help audiences ⑨ ____ what they ⑩ ____ on the ⑪ ____. Romantic music ⑫ ____ sweep the ⑬ ____ up in ⑭ ____ romantic moment. ⑮ ____ or intense ⑯ ____ can make ⑰ ____ scene in ⑱ ____ horror movie ⑲ ____ an adventure ⑳ ____ more exciting.

㉑ ____ consider this. ㉒ ____ are some ㉓ ____ and pieces ㉔ ____ music used ㉕ ____ movies that ㉖ ____ the power ㉗ ____ instantly bring ㉘ ____ of the ㉙ ____ back to ㉚ ____. Maybe it ㉛ ____ a song ㉜ ____ a movie ㉝ ____ we saw ㉞ ____ a child. ㉟ ____ we hear ㊱ ____ song today, ㊲ ____ remember the ㊳ ____. Maybe we ㊴ ____ even picture ㊵ ____ from the ㊶ ____ in our ㊷ ____. For example, ㊸ ____ song “Somewhere ㊹ ____ the Rainbow” ㊺ ____ most people think of *The* ㊻ ____ *of Oz*. ㊼ ____ maybe the ㊽ ____ string of ㊾ ____ do-re-㊿ ____-fa-so-(51) ____-ti-do (52) ____ you think (53) ____ *The Sound* (54) ____ *Music*.

There (55) ____ also plenty (56) ____ examples of (57) ____ without words (58) ____ the movies (59) ____ can bring (60) ____ mind titles (61) ____ scenes from (62) ____. You could (63) ____ easily recognize (64) ____ a few (65) ____ from the (66) ____ to *The* (67) ____ *Panther*. The (68) ____ is probably (69) ____ for the (70) ____ to the (71) ____ *Star Wars* (72) ____, in which (73) ____ Skywalker met (74) ____ Vader for (75) ____ first time. (76) ____ of my (77) ____ favorite movie (78) ____ come from (79) ____ movies *Jaws* (80) ____ the first (81) ____ Bond movie (82) ____ *No*. Just (83) ____ first two (84) ____ from the (85) ____ theme are (86) ____ for most (87) ____ to think (88) ____ a giant (89) ____ moving through (90) ____, dark water. (91) ____ I bet (92) ____ you asked (93) ____ of your (94) ____ to sing (95) ____ few bars (96) ____ the James (97) ____ theme, they (98) ____ do it. (99) ____ ahead and (100) ____.

Listening Test 🕘

PART I: Picture Description ((Track 112))

Listen and choose the statement that best describes what you see in the picture.

1.

    (A)   (B)   (C)   (D)

2.

    (A)   (B)   (C)   (D)

3.

    (A)   (B)   (C)   (D)

4.

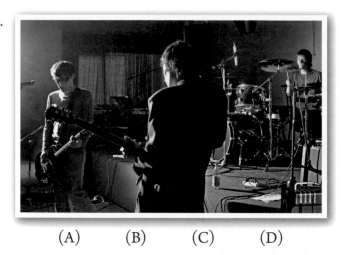

(A)   (B)   (C)   (D)

5.

(A)   (B)   (C)   (D)

PART II: Questions and Responses ((Track 113))

Listen and choose the best response to each question.

6. (A)   (B)   (C)

7. (A)   (B)   (C)

8. (A)   (B)   (C)

9. (A)   (B)   (C)

10. (A)   (B)   (C)

PART III: Short Conversations ((Track 114))

You will hear two dialogs, each followed by three questions. Listen carefully, and choose the best answer to each question.

11. What does the man want to know?

    (A) The easiest way to learn the guitar

    (B) The best guitar teacher in town

    (C) The fastest way to learn the guitar

    (D) The cheapest guitar teacher

12. What does the woman tell the man?

    (A) To find a good teacher

    (B) To practice every day

    (C) To find the best teacher

    (D) To find the most expensive teacher

13. Why does the woman recommend Michael?

    (A) He is the cheapest teacher in town.

    (B) He is the best guitar teacher in town.

    (C) He is an excellent teacher and his rates are cheaper.

    (D) He is the fastest teacher and his rates are good.

---

14. Why did the woman like the piano player?

    (A) Because he practiced every day

    (B) Because he sounded good

    (C) Because she loves the piano

    (D) Because he played with passion

15. What was the man's favorite part?

    (A) The duet

    (B) The piano player

    (C) The concert

    (D) The serious part

16. What did the man say about the duet?

    (A) He thought they sounded good together.

    (B) It was the worst thing he has ever heard.

    (C) He only liked the beginning.

    (D) He thought it was interesting.

PART IV: Short Talks (((Track 115)))

You will hear two talks, each followed by three questions. Listen carefully, and choose the best answer to each question.

17. What talent did the speaker not inherit?

    (A) His brother's strong voice

    (B) The ability to play soccer

    (C) His father's singing voice

    (D) His brother's good looks

18. What did everyone expect from the speaker's voice lessons?

    (A) That he would be a soccer player

    (B) That he would have a stronger voice than his brother

    (C) That he would be as good as his brother

    (D) That he would be a professional singer

19. What happened when the speaker played soccer?

    (A) He gave up after a few months.

    (B) He was the best player on his team.

    (C) He was very disappointed.

    (D) He didn't like it very much.

---

20. What is the speaker talking about?

    (A) YourMusic.com

    (B) Free streaming music

    (C) How to download MP3s

    (D) The best sites on the Internet

21. How much does it cost to download an MP3?

    (A) Nothing

    (B) 99 cents

    (C) More than one dollar

    (D) The cost is not mentioned.

22. What does the advertisement guarantee?

    (A) YourMusic.com has the hottest MP3 downloads.

    (B) YourMusic.com has the friendliest interface.

    (C) YourMusic.com is the fastest way to download songs.

    (D) YourMusic.com sells the cheapest musical instruments.

Groups

A

Look & Listen

Warm-up

Listen to the dialogs. Write the number next to the speakers. ((Track 116))

B

Listen Again

Listen again, and fill in the blanks. ((Track 117))

certain	not certain

1. The man is _____ they can beat the other team.
2. The man is _____ the district champions will win.
3. The speakers are _____ the seats are theirs.
4. The woman is _____ the racket is hers.

C

Essential Expressions

Sort the phrases into the right categories.

can't be	could be	couldn't be	has to be	may be
may not be	might be	might not be	must be	will be

Certain	Not Certain
_____	_____
_____	_____
_____	_____
_____	_____
_____	_____

Listening Practice

A

How would you answer?

Listen. Write the answer. ((Track 118))

> Actually, I am. Why are you surprised?   It could be, but it's hard to tell.
> They might actually win this year.   We may go camping.
>   Yes. She must be happy to get out of there.

1. _____
2. _____
3. _____
4. _____
5. _____

B

How would you ask?

Listen. Write the question. ((Track 119))

> Do you think the store is still open?   Did your registration expire?
> Why is that light on?   What colors should we use?
>   Can you guess who this present is for?

1. _____
2. _____
3. _____
4. _____
5. _____

C

Picture Description

Describe the picture using the words below.

| team | players |
| bench | watching |

_____
_____
_____

✓ **Listen to the description of the picture.** ((Track 120))

Speaking Practice

A

Pronunciation Practice

In casual speech, you may hear the phrase "lot of" pronounced as "lotta."

Written	Spoken
1. A lot of volunteers joined us.	1. A lotta volunteers joined us.
2. It was a lot of fun.	2. It was a lotta fun.
3. They have a lot of tips to share.	3. They have a lotta tips to share.

✓ **Now practice saying the following sentences.**

1. I made a lot of new friends.
2. She gave us a lot of help.
3. You can see a lot of players on the field.

✓ **Now listen and repeat.** ((Track 121))

B

Conversation Pictures

Listen to the dialogs, and number the pictures. ((Track 122))

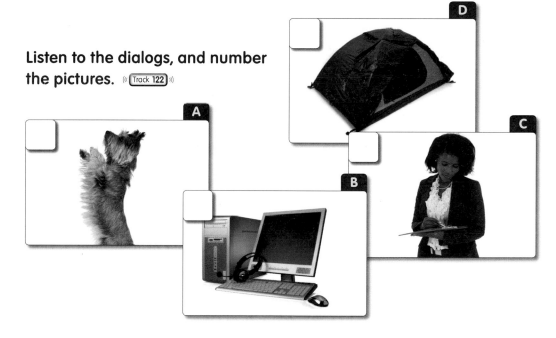

✓ **Now listen to the dialogs again, and choose the subject mentioned by the speakers.**

1. (A) club   (B) committee   (C) family   (D) organization
2. (A) club   (B) committee   (C) family   (D) organization
3. (A) club   (B) committee   (C) family   (D) organization
4. (A) club   (B) committee   (C) family   (D) organization

Short Dialogs

A

Dialog 1

Listen to the dialog and questions. Choose the best answer. ((Track 123))

1. (A) Their class   (B) Their club
   (C) Their co-workers   (D) Their sports team

2. (A) He doesn't know what the plant is. (B) He recognizes the flower.
   (C) He may take the plant home.   (D) He wants to give her a flower.

✓ **Listen again, and fill in the blanks.**

B: I love coming to the botanical garden in the
   ❶_____.

G: Me, too. Too ❷_____ we have to fill out this
   worksheet for ❸_____ while we're here.
   It kind of takes the ❹_____ out of our visit.

B: It's a small ❺_____ to pay. Hey, look! This
   flower ❻_____ be one of the orchids listed on
   our worksheet.

G: Oh, you're right. The name of the ❼_____ is
   on this sign. We can ❽_____ it from there.

B

Dialog 2

Listen to the dialog and questions. Choose the best answer. ((Track 124))

1. (A) Men's diving   (B) Men's volleyball
   (C) Women's gymnastics   (D) Women's racing

2. (A) They can't win.   (B) They could win gold.
   (C) They must need to rest.   (D) They will get first place.

C

Dialog 3

Listen to the dialog, and check (✓) the gifts that Tom will receive. ((Track 125))

1. ☐ Computer

2. ☐ DVD player

3. ☐ DVD

4. ☐ Movie tickets

Main Dialog

Listen to the dialog, and choose the best answer. ((Track 126))

1. What is the relationship of the speakers?
    (A) Classmates   (B) Co-workers
    (C) Strangers   (D) Volunteers

2. What is the group of volunteers doing?
    (A) Cleaning up the school grounds (B) Cutting the grass
    (C) Fixing a music store   (D) Planting things in the park

3. What does the boy imply about the change?
    (A) It can't be done any other day. (B) It may take several days.
    (C) It might require more volunteers. (D) It will save money.

Listen again, and fill in the blanks. ((Track 127))

W: Excuse me. I've been sitting on that ❶_____
over there watching you work. You look very ❷
_____ to me. Where have we met before?

M: I'm not sure. You might have seen me at my
part-time ❸_____. I work evening
and weekends at the ❹_____ store in
the mall.

W: That must have been where I've ❺_____ you before. What are you
guys doing to this part of the ❻_____?

M: We are taking out all the grass and replacing it with native
❼_____. It's a project that volunteers from our
❽_____ set up with the city government.

W: Why do you want to get rid of all the ❾_____?

M: There is a lot less maintenance and ❿_____
if the city puts in native plants here.

W: It must take you guys a long ⓫_____ to
cover this whole area with new plants.

M: Not really. A lot of volunteers came out to help today.
We should finish this ⓬_____.

Short Talks

A
Short Talk 1

Listen to the short talk and questions. Choose the best answer. ((Track 128))

1. (A) Change the bookstore (B) Elect a school leader
   (C) Get into the university (D) Sign up voters

2. (A) They could have forgotten. (B) They had to sign up first.
   (C) They might think it doesn't matter. (D) They must be busy.

✓ **Listen again, and fill in the blanks.**

The national election is coming up in a few ❶_____, so I joined an organization at my university that is working to get more students to ❷_____. Every time there is a national election, most university students don't ❸_____ to vote. Maybe they think it's a ❹_____ of time or that their vote won't ❺_____ for much. But that's not true. That's ❻_____ I volunteered to work at our organization's special ❼_____ in front of the bookstore. We're going to ask students to ❽_____ to vote and remind them how important their votes can be.

B
Short Talk 2

Listen to the short talk and questions. Choose the best answer. ((Track 129))

1. (A) Arizona (B) At school
   (C) In another country (D) Virginia

2. (A) They may play in the championships.
   (B) They will have tryouts in three weeks.
   (C) They can't win against her old team.
   (D) They could move to another city.

C
Short Talk 3

Listen to the short talk, and connect the object with its purpose. ((Track 130))

1. flashlight • • (A) to help get the treasure
2. long chopsticks • • (B) to see in the dark

A

Picture Matching

Listen to the dialogs. Choose the correct picture. ((Track 131))

 **A**

 **B**

 **C**

1. (A)   (B)   (C)

2. (A)   (B)   (C)

B

Listen & Choose

Listen to the dialogs and questions. Choose the best answer. ((Track 132))

3. (A) It couldn't be open.   (B) It has to be closed.
   (C) It might be open.   (D) It will be open only at night.

4. (A) They are on the same team.   (B) They injured another player.
   (C) They lost the game.   (D) They will play in the championship.

5. (A) Furniture shopping   (B) Making groups
   (C) School projects   (D) Their hobbies

6. (A) The boy's   (B) The girl's
   (C) Both the boy's and the girl's (D) Neither the boy's nor the girl's

7. (A) A light is on.   (B) A toy was put in the attic.
   (C) The light doesn't work.   (D) The show is finished.

8. (A) A neighbor's fence   (B) Part of the school
   (C) The man's room   (D) The woman's house

9. (A) He really likes the old color. (B) He thinks the paint is expensive.
   (C) He wants more than one color. (D) He would rather use a new color.

Wrap-up

A Pre-listening Discussion

Talk about these questions.

1. What was a group that you enjoyed being a part of?
2. How many people were in the group?
3. Who was the leader of the group?

B Listening Comprehension

Listen and answer the questions. Track 133

1. **What might be difficult about the storming stage?**

   ____.

2. **In which stage does a group do its best work?**

   ____.

3. **How many stages are described in basic group theory?**

   ____.

C Dictation Practice

Listen again, and fill in the blanks. Track 134

Think back ① ___ a time ② ___ you were ③ ___ of a ④ ___. Probably your ⑤ ___ went through ⑥ ___ couple of ⑦ ___ while you ⑧ ___ in it. ⑨ ___, the stages ⑩ ___ basic group ⑪ ___ are widely ⑫ ___ by people ⑬ ___ study groups ⑭ ___ schools, businesses, ⑮ ___ society.

According ⑯ ___ basic group ⑰ ___, the first ⑱ ___ a group ⑲ ___ through is ⑳ ___ the "forming" ㉑ ___. This is ㉒ ___ members of ㉓ ___ group first ㉔ ___ to know ㉕ ___ other. Usually ㉖ ___ group leader ㉗ ___ most of ㉘ ___ the group ㉙ ___ at this ㉚ ___. Members follow ㉛ ___ leader as ㉜ ___ learn what ㉝ ___ group does ㉞ ___ who the ㉟ ___ members are.

㊱ ___ comes the "㊲ ___" stage. This ㊳ ___ when group ㊴ ___ start to ㊵ ___ more control ㊶ ___ share their ㊷ ___. This is ㊸ ___ when groups ㊹ ___ have some ㊺ ___. Group members ㊻ ___ argue or ㊼ ___ fight during ㊽ ___ storming stage. ㊾ ___ sounds bad, ㊿ ___ it is (51) ___ normal and (52) ___ part of (53) ___ development.

If (54) ___ group can (55) ___ through the (56) ___ stage, they (57) ___ reach the (58) ___ called "norming." (59) ___ is when (60) ___ members solve (61) ___ problems they (62) ___ in the (63) ___ stage. They (64) ___ to work (65) ___, and the (66) ___ members form (67) ___ relationships with (68) ___ other.

Then (69) ___ the "performing" (70) ___. This is (71) ___ group members (72) ___ work by (73) ___, with a (74) ___ members, or (75) ___ the whole (76) ___. The group (77) ___ really get (78) ___ done at (79) ___ stage. Such (80) ___ can find (81) ___ ways to (82) ___ new problems (83) ___ work efficiently (84) ___ get projects (85) ___.

The last (86) ___ in basic (87) ___ theory is (88) ___ the group (89) ___ up. Of (90) ___, this can (91) ___ a tough (92) ___ for members, (93) ___ it is (94) ___ a time (95) ___ groups can (96) ___ members for (97) ___ great work (98) ___ did together.

Listening Test 🕘

PART I: Picture Description ((Track 135))

Listen and choose the statement that best describes what you see in the picture.

1.

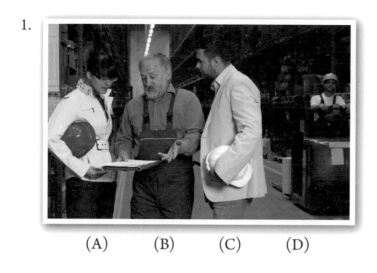

    (A)   (B)   (C)   (D)

2.

    (A)   (B)   (C)   (D)

3.

    (A)   (B)   (C)   (D)

4.

(A)   (B)   (C)   (D)

5.

(A)   (B)   (C)   (D)

PART II: Questions and Responses ((Track 136))

Listen and choose the best response to each question.

6. (A)   (B)   (C)

7. (A)   (B)   (C)

8. (A)   (B)   (C)

9. (A)   (B)   (C)

10. (A)   (B)   (C)

PART III: Short Conversations ((Track 137))

You will hear two dialogs, each followed by three questions. Listen carefully, and choose the best answer to each question.

11. What does the man think about the possible trip to Cancun?

    (A) The university won't allow it.

    (B) The woman is leaving tomorrow.

    (C) It's fantastic.

    (D) The club doesn't have enough money.

12. What is the rumor?

    (A) The club could be getting a huge donation.

    (B) Everyone wants to donate to the university.

    (C) The university is sending the club to Cancun.

    (D) The club is giving the university a donation.

13. What does the man say about the rumor?

    (A) It's too good to be true.

    (B) It's a huge donation.

    (C) It's not enough money.

    (D) It's too much money.

---

14. What can't the man believe?

    (A) That the Spurs are superstitious

    (B) That the Spurs won the game

    (C) That the Spurs lost the game

    (D) That he missed the game

15. Why does the woman think the Spurs lost?

    (A) Because of the team

    (B) Because of the place

    (C) Because of the man

    (D) Because of the date

16. Which is true about the man?

    (A) He thinks she may be right.

    (B) He wants to test her idea.

    (C) He doesn't agree with her.

    (D) He plans to do something silly.

PART IV: Short Talks (« Track 138 »)

You will hear two talks, each followed by three questions. Listen carefully, and choose the best answer to each question.

17. What is special about this weekend at the store?

    (A) It is a three-day weekend.
    (B) They have a much bigger staff.
    (C) Employees from another store are joining them.
    (D) The store is closed for a special reason.

18. What is the speaker's biggest concern?

    (A) That some staff members could be working in different areas
    (B) That they have enough cashiers at the main registers
    (C) That some areas might need extra support
    (D) That it will be too crowded

19. What does everyone have to do this weekend?

    (A) Learn how to work the cash registers
    (B) Work in a different section
    (C) Function as a team
    (D) Do a really good job

---

20. What does Dr. Richter say when the students ask about the final exam?

    (A) He will give them a copy of an old test.
    (B) They should make a study guide.
    (C) They have to be ready for a cumulative exam.
    (D) They should study alone.

21. What does the man wish Dr. Richter would make for the class?

    (A) An easy exam
    (B) A study guide
    (C) A cumulative exam
    (D) A better lesson plan

22. Why doesn't the speaker want to use his friends' study guide?

    (A) Because it may not include everything
    (B) Because he likes to study alone
    (C) Because he is crazy
    (D) Because they had an argument

Outdoors

Warm-up

Listen to the dialogs. Write the number next to the thing mentioned by the speakers. (Track 139)

Listen again, and fill in the note diagram with information from the dialogs. (Track 140)

What?	Location?
1. _____	in between _____
2. _____ / _____	ahead of _____ / next to _____
3. _____	on top of _____
4. _____	in front of _____

Circle the word or phrase that has a similar meaning.

1. across from = (far away from / not far from)
2. ahead of = (in front of / in back of)
3. at the end of = (on the other side of / to one side of)
4. close by = (near / under)
5. in between = (in the middle of / on top of)

Listening Practice

A

How would you answer?

Listen. Write the answer. ((Track 141))

> I think so.   There's one across from the hotel.   No, there isn't.
> Sure, I'd be happy to.   The one that leads away from the lake.

1. _____
2. _____
3. _____
4. _____
5. _____

B

How would you ask?

Listen. Write the question. ((Track 142))

> Where is the island?   Can you see their car?   Do you live around here?
> What is at the end of this block?   Is there a subway station around here?

1. _____
2. _____
3. _____
4. _____
5. _____

C

Picture Description

Describe the picture using the words below.

clouds	dome
fountain	water

_____
_____
_____
_____
_____

✓ **Listen to the description of the picture.** ((Track 143))

Speaking Practice

A
Intonation
Practice

In certain four-syllable statements or questions, the stress will usually be on the third syllable. Study the following statements and questions that typically have the stress pattern "dum dum da dum."

Written	Spoken
1. What's the matter?	1. What's the **mat**ter?
2. I'm so hungry.	2. I'm so **hun**gry.
3. I don't need one.	3. I don't **need** one.

✓ **Now practice saying the following sentences. Remember to stress the third syllable.**

1. Let's keep walking.
2. Can you see it?
3. Two little rabbits.

✓ **Now listen and repeat.** ((Track 144))

B
Conversation
Pictures

Listen to the dialogs, and number the pictures. ((Track 145))

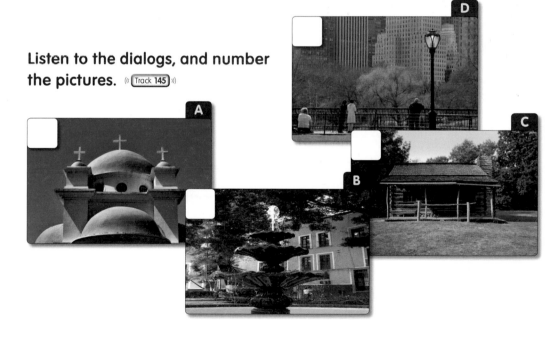

✓ **Now listen to the dialogs again, and choose the location mentioned by the speakers.**

1. (A) close to   (B) in back of   (C) on top of   (D) in the middle of
2. (A) close to   (B) in back of   (C) on top of   (D) in the middle of
3. (A) close to   (B) in back of   (C) on top of   (D) in the middle of
4. (A) close to   (B) in back of   (C) on top of   (D) in the middle of

Short Dialogs

Track 146

A

Dialog 1

Listen to the dialog and questions. Choose the best answer.

1. (A) Looking at a carousel   (B) Playing chess
   (C) Selling food   (D) Walking in the park

2. (A) Across the pond   (B) Close to the carousel
   (C) In between the tables   (D) Just ahead of them

✓ **Listen again, and fill in the blanks.**

M: There's a place for people to ❶_____ chess and checkers. Do you want to walk ❷_____ there?

W: Sure. It looks like there's a pond ❸_____ by there, too. Can you see it on the other ❹_____ of those trees?

M: Oh, yeah. I see it. After we walk ❺_____ the chess and checker area, we can follow that ❻_____ over to the carousel.

W: Maybe we'll see someone selling coffee and donuts ❼_____ the way. I'm getting kind of hungry.

W: If not, I know that there's a restaurant right ❽_____ from the carousel.

B

Dialog 2

Listen to the dialog and questions. Choose the best answer. Track 147

1. (A) For exercise   (B) For their job
   (C) To get around   (D) To save money

2. (A) A restroom   (B) His favorite roller coaster
   (C) Something to drink   (D) The arcade

C

Dialog 3

Listen to the dialog and questions. Complete the answers. Track 148

1. She used _____ inside the _____.
2. She suggests _____ a pole on top of _____.

Main Dialog

Listen to the dialog, and choose the best answer. ((Track 149))

1. What can be inferred about the speakers?
   - (A) They are tour guides.
   - (B) They are tourists.
   - (C) They live by the ocean.
   - (D) They work on the trolley.

2. What does the man want to see in the Gaslamp Quarter?
   - (A) A block with expensive homes
   - (B) A place with historical things
   - (C) A special kind of store
   - (D) A street with performers

3. Which place is NOT mentioned by the speakers?
   - (A) A famous restaurant
   - (B) A historic area
   - (C) A market area
   - (D) A museum

Listen again, and fill in the blanks. ((Track 150))

W: It's fun to ride around on the trolley and see different ❶_____ of the city.

M: Do you want to get off the trolley ❷_____ the Ocean Beach Farmers' Market and see what they have?

W: OK. I think the antique ❸_____ is at the end of that same ❹_____.

M: Why don't we ❺_____ at the antique district and work our way down toward the ❻_____?

W: Good idea.

M: Wait a minute. This street looks ❼_____. I think this is the Gaslamp Quarter. Let's ❽_____ of the trolley here.

W: What's there to see ❾_____?

M: It's a historic district, so there are lots of buildings from the 1800s. There is also a cool ❿_____ not far from here that I want to ⓫_____.

W: You go ahead. I'm going to go into the art ⓬_____ that's right next to the trolley stop.

Short Talks

Listen to the short talk and questions. Choose the best answer. ((Track 151))

1. (A) Between two cities
   (C) In back of a famous building
   (B) By her office
   (D) Near her home

2. (A) It goes along the river.
   (C) It is crowded at lunch time.
   (B) It is closed in the morning.
   (D) It is far from the river.

✓ **Listen again, and fill in the blanks.**

I'm lucky to ❶_____ in a place with a small river close by my ❷_____ building. When the city built the ❸_____ and sidewalks around this area, they put in a jogging and bike riding trail ❹_____ the river. Lots of people in the area where I ❺_____ enjoy walking and exercising along this trail. Lots of ❻_____ can usually be seen out by the river in the ❼_____ after work. Personally, I prefer to do my exercising in the ❽_____, so that's when I go out and jog on the trail along the river.

B

Short Talk 2

Listen to the short talk and questions. Choose the best answer. ((Track 152))

1. (A) A 30-minute boat ride away
   (C) Too far away to see
   (B) Fairly close by
   (D) In between a larger island and the coast

2. (A) Across from the island
   (C) On the beach
   (B) Inside of a cabin
   (D) On top of a hill

C

Short Talk 3

Listen to the short talk, and fill in the missing information on the map. ((Track 15

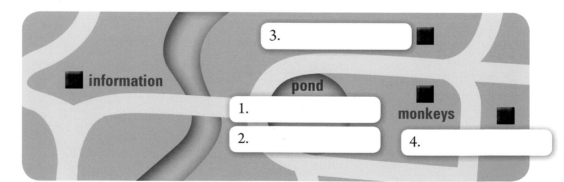

Listening Quiz 04:47

A

Picture Matching

Listen to the dialogs. Choose the correct picture. ((Track 154))

1. (A)　　　　(B)　　　　(C)

2. (A)　　　　(B)　　　　(C)

B

Listen & Choose

Listen to the dialogs and questions. Choose the best answer. ((Track 155))

3. (A) Across from the hotel　　(B) At his family's gift shop
   (C) At the airport　　(D) In the hotel lobby

4. (A) Eat　　(B) Help a friend
   (C) Practice with the choir　　(D) Shop

5. (A) They are camping.　　(B) They are lost.
   (C) They have a trail map.　　(D) They need wood.

6. (A) At an outdoor market　　(B) At the zoo
   (C) In her house　　(D) In his yard

7. (A) In back of her　　(B) In his hand
   (C) On a log　　(D) Up a tree

8. (A) A car sales lot　　(B) A parking garage
   (C) Her garage　　(D) The highway

9. (A) A blue light post　　(B) A red truck
   (C) The aisle number　　(D) The male speaker

Wrap-up

A
Pre-listening
Discussion

B
Listening
Comprehension

C
Dictation
Practice

Talk about these questions.

1. Where is the largest city park in your hometown?
2. What can people see or do at that park?
3. What do you know about Central Park?

Listen and answer the questions. ((Track 156))

1. **In which part of the park can you find Bethesda Fountain?**

_____

2. **Which two parts of the park does Bow Bridge connect?**

_____

3. **In which part of the park can the largest lake be found?**

_____

Listen again, and fill in the blanks. ((Track 157))

If you ❶_____ happen to ❷_____ yourself in ❸_____ York City, ❹____ would highly ❺_____ a visit ❻____ Central Park. ❼____ course, visiting ❽_____ Park isn't ❾_____ like visiting ❿_____ in other ⓫_____. For one ⓬_____, Central Park ⓭____ huge! Also, ⓮_____ you enter ⓯_____ Park, there ⓰_____ lots of ⓱_____ things you ⓲_____ see and ⓳____.

In the ⓴_____ part of ㉑_____ park, you ㉒_____ find Bethesda ㉓_____. No doubt ㉔_____ you visit ㉕_____ spot, you ㉖_____ recognize the ㉗_____ standing in ㉘_____ of you. ㉙_____ movies have �30_____ filmed here, �31____ the statue �32_____ the fountain �33_____ well known �34_____ appearing in �35_____. There is �36_____ a place �37_____ where people �38_____ stand and �39_____ out over �40____ lake.

Another ㊶_____ in Central ㊷_____ that is ㊸_____ seen in ㊹_____ is close ㊺____ Bethesda Fountain. ㊻_____ Bow Bridge. ㊼_____ due east ㊽_____ Bethesda Fountain ㊾_____ Cherry Hill ㊿_____ then walk ⑤①_____ from Cherry ⑤②_____ to find ⑤③_____ bridge. When ⑤④_____ get to ⑤⑤_____ Bridge, you ⑤⑥_____ see a ⑤⑦_____ of the ⑤⑧_____ that is ⑤⑨_____ The Ramble ⑥⓪_____ of you ⑥①____ the other ⑥②_____ of the ⑥③_____. The Ramble ⑥④____ a kind ⑥⑤____ wild part ⑥⑥____ the park ⑥⑦_____ is fun ⑥⑧____ wander through. ⑥⑨_____ can forget ⑦⓪_____ in the ⑦①_____ of New ⑦②_____ City in ⑦③_____!

These are ⑦④_____ a few ⑦⑤_____ spots in ⑦⑥_____ south part ⑦⑦____ Central Park. ⑦⑧_____ are still ⑦⑨_____ of things ⑧⓪____ see in ⑧①_____ north part. ⑧②____ fact, the ⑧③_____ lake in ⑧④_____ Park is ⑧⑤____ the north ⑧⑥_____. That is ⑧⑦_____ everyone should ⑧⑧_____ see on ⑧⑨____ trip to ⑨⓪_____ York's Central ⑨①_____.

Listening Test ^{08:56}

PART I: Picture Description (((Track 158)))

Listen and choose the statement that best describes what you see in the picture.

1.

(A)   (B)   (C)   (D)

2.

(A)   (B)   (C)   (D)

3.

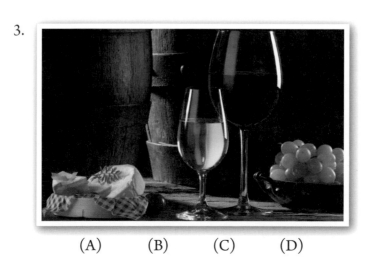

(A)   (B)   (C)   (D)

4.

(A)   (B)   (C)   (D)

5.

(A)   (B)   (C)   (D)

PART II: Questions and Responses ((Track 159))

Listen and choose the best response to each question.

6. (A)   (B)   (C)

7. (A)   (B)   (C)

8. (A)   (B)   (C)

9. (A)   (B)   (C)

10. (A)   (B)   (C)

PART III: Short Conversations ((Track 160))

You will hear two dialogs, each followed by three questions. Listen carefully, and choose the best answer to each question.

11. Where is Margaret going?
    - (A) To the museum
    - (B) To a picnic in the park
    - (C) Around the corner
    - (D) In front of the man

12. Where is the park?
    - (A) Far from here
    - (B) By the museum
    - (C) Around the corner
    - (D) On a hill

13. What is between the museum and the library?
    - (A) A park
    - (B) A picnic
    - (C) A store
    - (D) The speakers

14. Where are the man and woman going?
    - (A) To the zoo
    - (B) To the botanical garden
    - (C) To the gas station
    - (D) To the river

15. Where is their destination?
    - (A) At the zoo
    - (B) Next to the zoo
    - (C) Between the garden and the river
    - (D) In front of the zoo

16. When does the woman go there?
    - (A) Very seldom
    - (B) When the man invites her
    - (C) Every weekend
    - (D) Most days

PART IV: Short Talks ((Track 161))

You will hear two talks, each followed by three questions. Listen carefully, and choose the best answer to each question.

17. Where are the members of the group?

    (A) At a picnic
    (B) On a hill
    (C) At a camp
    (D) Near the lake

18. Where will the group stop for lunch?

    (A) In front of a patch of wildflowers
    (B) Between the mountains and a lake
    (C) Near a very old bridge
    (D) Between the camp and the top of the mountain

19. Which of the following does the speaker NOT mention doing?

    (A) Hiking up the mountain
    (B) Crossing a bridge
    (C) Swimming in the lake
    (D) Taking pictures

---

20. What is the speaker doing?

    (A) Giving directions
    (B) Drawing a map
    (C) Suggesting a plan
    (D) Remembering her hometown

21. Where is the ice cream parlor located?

    (A) Next to the woman's house
    (B) Next to a clothing store
    (C) Across from the theater
    (D) On the way back

22. Where is the woman's house?

    (A) By the bank
    (B) Between the movie theater and the bank
    (C) Downtown
    (D) Across from a restaurant

Meetings

Warm-up

A
Look & Listen

Listen to the dialogs. Write the number next to the person who makes an announcement or suggestion. ((Track 162))

B
Listen Again

Listen again, and fill in the blanks. ((Track 163))

1. Gloria announces that Student Services _____.
2. Nancy announces that the club _____.
3. Kevin suggests that they _____ or they
   _____.
4. Jim suggests that they _____.

C
Essential Expressions

Fill in the blanks with the right word or phrase from the box.

| a little less | at least | fewer | fewest | less than |
| more | much more | the least | the most | the same |

1. The art club has the _____ members.
2. The English club gets _____ money than the art club.
3. All of the clubs have _____ ten members.
4. The art club's budget is _____ the math club's budget.
5. The English club has _____ number of meetings per month.
6. One club has _____ meetings than the other clubs.
7. The math club has _____ members than the English club.
8. Two clubs have _____ number of meetings each month.
9. The math club gets _____ money than the other clubs.
10. The math club has _____ members.

Art Club
10 members
$300/yr
4 meetings/month

Math Club
28 members
$500/yr
4 meetings/month

English Club
25 members
$290/yr
2 meetings/month

Listening Practice

How would you answer?

Listen. Write the answer. ((Track 164))

> I doubt that will be possible.   Indeed, it does.   The Latin club.
> We will receive less money.   Yes, I think sales has more bad news for us.

1. _____
2. _____
3. _____
4. _____
5. _____

B

How would you ask?

Listen. Write the question. ((Track 165))

> Is everyone here yet?   Does anyone have any other ideas?
> Will this room be large enough?   What if fewer people join the club?
>   Are you going to join the study group?

1. _____
2. _____
3. _____
4. _____
5. _____

C

Picture Description

Describe the picture using the words below.

ground	more women
outdoors	studying

_____
_____
_____
_____

✓ **Listen to the description of the picture.** ((Track 166))

Speaking Practice

A

Pronunciation Practice

Reduced speech is common in casual speech. You may hear the phrase "lot of" pronounced as "lotta" many times.

Written	Spoken
1. There are a lot of things we can do. 2. A lot of people had to go study. 3. We have a lot of drinks already.	1. There are a lotta things we can do. 2. A lotta people had to go study. 3. We have a lotta drinks already.

✓ **Now practice saying the following sentence, as you did in Unit 6.**

1. It will be a lot of fun.
2. I think that is happening to a lot of other clubs.
3. We planned a lot of events for the coming months.

✓ **Now listen and repeat.** ((Track 167))

B

Conversation Pictures

Listen to the dialogs, and number the pictures. ((Track 168))

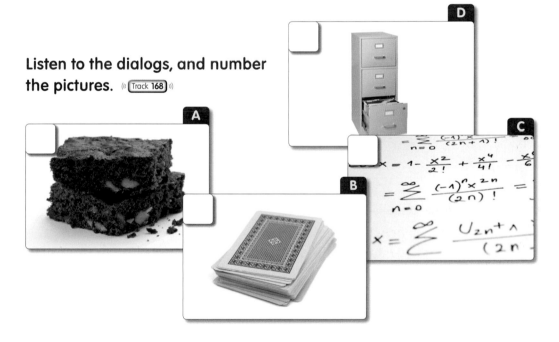

✓ **Now listen to the dialogs again, and choose the correct group or organization mentioned by the speakers.**

1. (A) Club   (B) Friends   (C) Office   (D) Study group
2. (A) Club   (B) Friends   (C) Office   (D) Study group
3. (A) Club   (B) Friends   (C) Office   (D) Study group
4. (A) Club   (B) Friends   (C) Office   (D) Study group

Short Dialogs

Listen to the dialog and questions. Choose the best answer. ((Track 169))

1. (A) Daily   (B) Weekly
   (C) Monthly   (D) Less than once a month

2. (A) Food   (B) Players
   (C) The game   (D) The TV

✓ **Listen again, and fill in the blanks.**

W: Hey, Ted. What's up? How come you're
   ❶_____ so late?

M: I was calling to ask if we could have this
   ❷_____ mahjongg game at your place
tomorrow night. Our TV is broken.

W: Our place? We just had it here ❸_____
week. I'd really rather not host back-to-back
mahjongg ❹_____ here. Don't worry
about the ❺_____.

M: But everyone likes to have the TV on while we're
❻_____.

W: It's no big deal, Ted. The most ❼_____
things are the food, the game, and the
❽_____. We can listen to CDs instead.

Listen to the dialog and questions. Choose the best answer. ((Track 170))

1. (A) It has a big budget.   (B) It has fewer meetings.
   (C) It has high membership dues.   (D) It has lots of members.

2. (A) The Latin Club   (B) The Poetry Club
   (C) The Ski Club   (D) The Speakers' Club

Listen to the dialog, and check (✓) the information that can be inferred from what is said. ((Track 171))

1. ☐ There are two girls and two boys in the group.
   ☐ There are three girls and one boy in the group.

2. ☐ The speakers are in the library.
   ☐ The speakers will go to the library after their class.

Main Dialog

Listen to the dialog, and choose the best answer. ((Track 172))

1. What was suggested at this meeting?
   - (A) Approving management's plan
   - (B) Electing a vice president
   - (C) Hiring another person
   - (D) Setting up a website

2. Who is being promoted?
   - (A) Brad
   - (B) Mark
   - (C) Nancy
   - (D) Mark and Nancy

3. How do the people at the meeting react to the announcement?
   - (A) They are amused.
   - (B) They are annoyed.
   - (C) They are glad.
   - (D) They are shocked.

Listen again, and fill in the blanks. ((Track 173))

M₁: May I make a suggestion at this point? I think we need one ❶_____ salesperson. We are sure to increase ❷_____ with more salespeople.

W₁: I agree with Brad. And I think we need a full-time staff ❸_____ to keep up with our department's website.

W₂: Those are excellent ❹_____. Any other ideas?

M₁: I can think of a few more things, but they are ❺_____ important than another salesperson and a webmaster.

W₂: All right then, I'll take these suggestions ❻_____ to management for approval.

M₁: How long will it be ❼_____ we know for sure?

W₂: Less than a week. And I have one more important announcement. I am being ❽_____ to vice president, and Mark will be ❾_____ to take my place.

M₂: Well, we all know no one can take Nancy's place, but I'll try to do the ❿_____ damage possible.

W₁: Congratulations! That is great. No one deserves a promotion more than you ⓫_____.

M₁: I couldn't agree more. Let's go out to ⓬_____ to celebrate.

Short Talks

A
Short Talk 1

Listen to the short talk and questions. Choose the best answer. ((Track 174))

1. (A) Just Tom
   (C) Three
   (B) Two
   (D) Four

2. (A) She does well in this subject.
   (C) She needs help in this subject.
   (B) She might fail the class.
   (D) She took the test before.

✓ **Listen again, and fill in the blanks.**

Hi, Tom. I'm calling to see if you would be interested in joining a study group for ❶_____. I'm kind of worried about the test that is coming up in ❷_____ weeks. I didn't do very well on the ❸_____ test, so I've got to get at least an ❹_____ on the upcoming test. I've already asked Sandra if she would be interested in ❺_____ a study group. She said she would. You know she never gets less than an ❻_____ on her math exams. So give me a call and let me know if ❼_____ want to join our study group. I'll talk to you ❽_____. Bye.

B
Short Talk 2

Listen to the short talk and questions. Choose the best answer. ((Track 175))

1. (A) The room's availability
   (C) The room's size
   (B) The room's noise
   (D) The room's whiteboard

2. (A) Not very long
   (C) Not more than two hours
   (B) About one hour
   (D) Possibly more than two hours

C
Short Talk 3

Listen to the short talk, and number the hands in order from 1 (the least number of points) to 4 (the most number of points). ((Track 176))

_____ (A) No hearts + no spades

_____ (B) Only the king of hearts

_____ (C) Only the queen of spades

_____ (D) The eight of hearts + the king of hearts

Listen to the dialogs. Choose the correct picture. ((Track 177))

 A  B  C

1. (A)   (B)   (C)

2. (A)   (B)   (C)

Listen to the dialogs and questions. Choose the best answer. ((Track 178))

3. (A) Fundraising activities   (B) New members
   (C) Social activities   (D) The budget

4. (A) A coffee shop   (B) Phil and Cathy's house
   (C) Ted and Monica's house   (D) The supermarket

5. (A) Buyer and seller   (B) Co-workers
   (C) Husband and wife   (D) Teacher and student

6. (A) None will be office assistants   (B) One will be an office assistant
   (C) Two will be office assistants   (D) All will be office assistants

7. (A) Losing money   (B) Most stressful
   (C) Very productive   (D) Newest department in the company

8. (A) Completing a group project   (B) Reviewing for a test
   (C) Sharing notes from the lecture   (D) Working on an assignment

9. (A) The man   (B) The woman
   (C) Both the man and the woman   (D) Neither the man nor the woman

A
Pre-listening
Discussion

B
Listening
Comprehension

C
Dictation
Practice

Wrap-up

Talk about these questions.

1. What was the last meeting you went to?
2. How many people were at that meeting?
3. How long did the meeting last?

Listen and answer the questions. ((Track 179))

1. **For sharing information, which is better: having a meeting or sending an email?**
   _____

2. **Who should not be invited to a meeting?**
   _____

3. **What are all of these suggestions aiming to do?**
   _____

Listen again, and fill in the blanks. ((Track 180))

The next ❶_____ you have ❷____ plan and ❸_____ a meeting, ❹_____ should try ❺____ couple of ❻_____ things to ❼_____ the meeting ❽_____ more smoothly. ❾_____ are just ❿_____ ideas to ⓫_____ you and ⓬_____ other people ⓭_____ get the ⓮_____ out of ⓯_____ meeting. The ⓰_____ thing I ⓱_____ suggest is ⓲____ really think ⓳_____ the purpose ⓴____ the meeting. ㉑_____ can ask ㉒_____ this question: "㉓____ we need ㉔____ have this ㉕_____ at all?" ㉖_____ you just ㉗_____ to share ㉘_____ with people. ㉙___ you need ㉚____ do that ㉛____ a meeting? ㉜_____ you could ㉝_____ the information ㉞_____ emails or ㉟_____ calls. The ㊱_____ here is ㊲_____ if you ㊳_____ avoid calling ㊴____ meeting, you ㊵_____. Meetings take ㊶_____ away from ㊷_____ schedules. If you ㊸_____ achieve the ㊹_____ of the ㊺_____ without really ㊻_____ the meeting, ㊼_____ it's better ㊽____ do it without the meeting.

㊾____ second suggestion ㊿____ to carefully 51_____ who you 52_____ invite to 53_____ meeting. Only 54_____ the people 55_____ really need 56____ be there. 57____ someone on 58_____ list isn't 59_____ to give 60_____ information, vote 61_____ something, or 62_____ a role 63____ the meeting, 64_____ don't invite 65_____ or her. 66_____, that person 67_____ appreciate not 68_____ required to 69_____ to the 70_____. You're respecting 71_____ person's time 72____ not inviting 73_____ or her. 74____ for any 75_____ you have, 76_____ call people 77_____ really need 78____ be there.

79_____ good thing 80____ keep in 81_____ is the 82_____ and ending 83_____ of the 84_____. Do your 85_____ to start 86____ time and 87_____ on time. 88_____ goes back 89____ that idea 90____ respecting people's 91_____. The more 92_____ respect their 93_____, the more 94_____ will respect 95_____ as a 96_____.

Listening Test 🕘 09:43

PART I: Picture Description ((Track 181))

Listen and choose the statement that best describes what you see in the picture.

1.

    (A)   (B)   (C)   (D)

2.

    (A)   (B)   (C)   (D)

3.

    (A)   (B)   (C)   (D)

4.

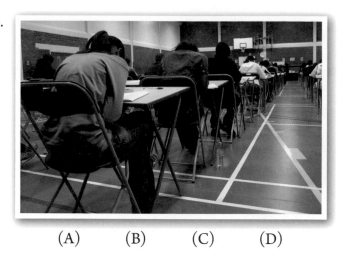

(A)   (B)   (C)   (D)

5.

(A)   (B)   (C)   (D)

PART II: Questions and Responses ((Track 182))

Listen and choose the best response to each question.

6. (A)   (B)   (C)

7. (A)   (B)   (C)

8. (A)   (B)   (C)

9. (A)   (B)   (C)

10. (A)   (B)   (C)

PART III: Short Conversations ((Track 183))

You will hear two dialogs, each followed by three questions. Listen carefully, and choose the best answer to each question.

11. What bad news did the students receive?

   (A) They are not getting $500.
   (B) Their club was closed.
   (C) Their attendance is down from previous semesters.
   (D) The school will give them less money than before.

12. How does the woman feel about the news about the budget?

   (A) Not surprised
   (B) Angry
   (C) Confused
   (D) Pleased

13. How can the club save some money?

   (A) They can cut at least $500 from the cost of activities.
   (B) They can get more members.
   (C) They can do activities that are less expensive.
   (D) They can hold fewer meetings during the semester.

14. What is the man surprised about?

   (A) He saw a friend unexpectedly.
   (B) He was not expecting an invitation.
   (C) It is time to play cards again.
   (D) The woman knew all the information.

15. How often does the group get together to do their activity?

   (A) Once a week
   (B) Every other Wednesday
   (C) Several times a week
   (D) Most weekends

16. Why will the woman call Larry?

   (A) She wants to play cards.
   (B) She is going to his house.
   (C) She wants to confirm the plan.
   (D) She wants to know what time the reunion will be.

PART IV: Short Talks ((Track 184))

You will hear two talks, each followed by three questions. Listen carefully, and choose the best answer to each question.

17. What is this advertisement about?

    (A) Making money by working for representatives
    (B) An informational meeting about a business opportunity
    (C) The exciting new facilities at a resort hotel
    (D) Job openings at the Summit Hotel

18. What time will the meeting end?

    (A) Before 2:00
    (B) Around 4:00
    (C) Between 6:00 and 7:00
    (D) By at least 6:00

19. Who is invited to the meeting?

    (A) The Summit Hotel staff
    (B) People who need a job
    (C) People who are really interested
    (D) Company representatives

---

20. What is the purpose of this message?

    (A) To advise of a room change
    (B) To invite students to study
    (C) To give directions to the Chemistry department
    (D) To encourage students to study for their exam

21. Where will the meeting take place?

    (A) In the cafeteria
    (B) In the school's library
    (C) In the Chemistry department study room
    (D) In the lobby of the Chemistry department

22. Where will next week's meeting be?

    (A) In the lobby of the Chemistry department
    (B) In the library
    (C) Outside the department
    (D) The location has not yet been announced.

Feelings

Warm-up

A
Look & Listen

Listen to the dialogs. Write the number next to the speakers. ((Track 185))

B
Listen Again

Listen again, and circle the right word. ((Track 186))

1. The woman is (annoyed / confused).
2. The man is (cheerful / sorry).
3. The man is (glad / upset).
4. The woman is (pleased / worried).

C
Essential Expressions

Sort the words and phrases into the right categories.

annoyed	glad	disappointed	cheerful	excited
disgusted	upset	appreciative	embarrassed	jealous
furious	pleased	looking forward to		

Positive feelings

_____

_____

_____

_____

_____

Negative feelings

_____

_____

_____

_____

_____

Listening Practice

Listen. Write the answer. ((Track 187))

> Actually, I can't go.　　　I was disgusted.　　　You certainly did!
> Maybe he is just jealous.　　　　　　　　　It was my pleasure.

1. _____

2. _____

3. _____

4. _____

5. _____

Listen. Write the question. ((Track 188))

> Where have you been?　　　　　　How was your test score?
> Why do you look so worried?　　　　Why did her face turn red?
> 　　　　Were you depressed about losing your job?

1. _____

2. _____

3. _____

4. _____

5. _____

Describe the picture using the words below.

> happy　　　　pointing
> smiling　　　serious

_____

_____

_____

_____

✓ **Listen to the description of the picture.** ((Track 189))

Speaking Practice

A

Intonation
Practice

In certain four-syllable statements or questions, the stress will usually be on the second syllable. Study the following statements and questions that typically have the stress pattern "dum da dum dum."

Written	Spoken
1. That's no excuse.	1. That's **no** excuse.
2. He worked on it.	2. He **worked** on it.
3. It wasn't me.	3. It **was**n't me.

✓ Now practice saying the following sentences. Remember to stress the second syllable.

1. What time is it?
2. That's terrible.
3. I'm so sorry.

✓ **Now listen and repeat.** ((Track 190))

B

Conversation
Pictures

Listen to the dialogs, and number the pictures. ((Track 191))

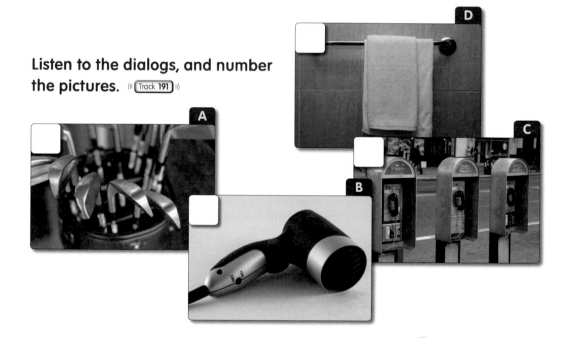

✓ **Now listen to the dialogs again, and choose the feeling mentioned by the speakers.**

1. (A) appreciative (B) disappointed (C) furious (D) surprised
2. (A) appreciative (B) disappointed (C) furious (D) surprised
3. (A) appreciative (B) disappointed (C) furious (D) surprised
4. (A) appreciative (B) disappointed (C) furious (D) surprised

Short Dialogs

A

Dialog 1

Listen to the dialog and questions. Choose the best answer. ((Track 192))

1. (A) Graphs
   (C) Presentation notes
   (B) Letters
   (D) Reports

2. (A) Her help with a presentation
   (C) Her offer to help with the project
   (B) Her help with the reports
   (D) Her offer to meet another day

✓ Listen again, and fill in the blanks.

W: Hi. I came to collect those ❶_____ you said you'd have ready for me.

M: Sure, here they are. Do you need any ❷_____ with that project you're working on?

W: No, I don't think ❸_____. I think I have everything I need.

M: Are you sure? I'd be ❹_____ to help. I still owe you one for helping me out with those ❺_____ for my presentation. I really appreciate ❻_____ you did for me.

W: Oh, don't mention it. You don't ❼_____ me a thing. Thanks for the ❽_____, though!

B

Dialog 2

Listen to the dialog and questions. Choose the best answer. ((Track 193))

1. (A) Another person
   (C) The male speaker
   (B) The female speaker
   (D) The two speakers

2. (A) Nick is jealous about her promotion.
   (C) Nick thinks she is always kind.
   (B) Nick is happy for her.
   (D) Nick's feelings were hurt by her.

C

Dialog 3

Listen to the dialog, and choose the right word to complete each sentence. ((Track 194))

1. The woman is (disappointed / pleased) with her roommate.
2. The man is (amused / disgusted) by his roommate.

Main Dialog

A
Listen

Listen to the dialog, and choose the best answer. ((Track 195))

1. What is Carol sorry about?
   - (A) Being late
   - (B) Mike's situation
   - (C) Not meeting more often
   - (D) Working too much

2. How does Mike feel at the moment?
   - (A) Angry
   - (B) Delighted
   - (C) Depressed
   - (D) Satisfied

3. Which of the following is true about Mike at the moment?
   - (A) He has a family.
   - (B) He has a job.
   - (C) He has his own company.
   - (D) He has to move.

B
Listen Again

Listen again, and fill in the blanks. ((Track 196))

W: Hi, Mike. I haven't ❶_____ you around for a while.

M: Hi, Carol. I guess you didn't hear that I ❷_____ my job about a week ago.

W: Oh, no! I'm so ❸_____! That's awful!

M: Well, maybe a week ago, I would have ❹_____ with you. But now, I don't think so at all.

W: What do you ❺_____?

M: Let me explain. At first, I was very ❻_____, which is not surprising. But now, I've begun to ❼_____ that what seems to be a disaster could actually be a ❽_____ opportunity.

W: A blessing in disguise, you mean?

M: Yes, that's right. Being laid off might not be such a ❾_____ thing after all. I can't say that I'm really ❿_____ that this happened to me, but I'm going to take some time off to spend with my ⓫_____. I'm also thinking about trying to start my own ⓬_____.

Short Talks

A

Short Talk 1

Listen to the short talk and questions. Choose the best answer. ((Track 197))

1. (A) Deleted the message
   (C) Sent an email
   (B) Met the writer
   (D) Talked to a friend

2. (A) The comments were clever.
   (C) The speaker was mistaken.
   (B) The message was offensive.
   (D) The writer was still angry.

✓ **Listen again, and fill in the blanks.**

I recently received a rather ❶_____ email from someone that I know. The person isn't a ❷_____ friend of mine, but I have met her several times through my other friends. The first time that I read this person's email, I actually got a little ❸_____. I wanted to write her back right away, but I didn't. I talked to a close ❹_____ of mine about the email. She asked to read the email. She thought I had the ❺_____ impression about what it said. My friend ❻_____ I got offended by something that was not meant in a ❼_____ way at all. Sometimes, it's hard to read the real feelings ❽_____ certain comments made in emails.

B

Short Talk 2

Listen to the short talk and questions. Choose the best answer. ((Track 198))

1. (A) Cooking breakfast together
   (C) The place and the people
   (B) Food and fun
   (D) The morning his grandmother arrived

2. (A) Cheerful
   (C) Serious
   (B) Embarrassing
   (D) Worried

C

Short Talk 3

Listen to the short talk and questions. Complete the answers. ((Track 199))

1. After Spot died, _____.
2. They noticed that _____.

Listening Quiz

05:42

Listen to the dialogs. Choose the correct picture. ((Track 200))

A

B

C

A
Picture Matching

B
Listen & Choose

1. (A)   (B)   (C)

2. (A)   (B)   (C)

Listen to the dialogs and questions. Choose the best answer. ((Track 201))

3. (A) She didn't want to attend.   (B) She forgot to attend.
   (C) She hopes he can attend.   (D) She wanted to attend.

4. (A) He liked it before.   (B) He never liked it.
   (C) He only likes it in restaurants.   (D) He would like it for dinner.

5. (A) A co-worker   (B) A stranger
   (C) The man   (D) The waiter

6. (A) A dating couple   (B) Brother and sister
   (C) Co-workers   (D) Teacher and student

7. (A) Her father   (B) Her friends
   (C) The girl   (D) Tom

8. (A) Management couldn't attend.   (B) The man couldn't attend.
   (C) The woman couldn't attend.   (D) Nobody could attend.

9. (A) Meeting a new employee   (B) Missing the meeting
   (C) Reading the memo   (D) Speaking to the manager

Wrap-up

Talk about these questions.

1. Who do you know that complains a lot?
2. Would it be difficult to go for a whole week without complaining?
3. Why do people wear awareness bracelets?

Listen and answer the questions. ((Track 202))

1. **Who had the idea to use bracelets to remind people not to complain?**

   _____

2. **What do people wearing the bracelets have to do if they complain?**

   _____

3. **How can people get these bracelets?**

   _____

Listen again, and fill in the blanks. ((Track 203))

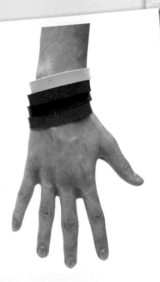

I have **1**_____ that I **2**_____ a lot. **3**_____, I've noticed **4**____ complain now **5**_____ I'm trying **6**_____ to complain.

7_____ of my **8**_____ at school **9**_____ a kind **10**____ experiment called "**11**____ Complaint Free **12**_____." The idea **13**_____ this experiment **14**_____ from an **15**_____ we read **16**____ a magazine. **17**_____ article was **18**_____ a pastor **19**_____ the United **20**_____ who asked **21**_____ of the **22**_____ in his **23**_____ to try **24**____ stop complaining **25**_____ 21 days. **26**_____ he also **27**_____ them to **28**_____ track of **29**_____ days very **30**_____. All of **31**_____ people in **32**_____ church were **33**_____ to wear **34**____ purple rubber **35**_____. Any time **36**____ person complained, **37**____ or she **38**_____ to move **39**_____ bracelet from **40**_____ wrist to **41**_____ other and **42**_____ counting days **43**_____ from zero. **44**_____ article said **45**____ took the **46**_____ over three **47**_____ of trying **48**_____ to complain **49**_____ he could **50**____ 21 straight **51**_____ without a complaint.

The idea **52**____ using the **53**_____ bracelets to **54**_____ people not **55**____ complain really **56**_____ on. In **57**_____, it started **58**____ whole new **59**_____ called A **60**_____ Free World. **61**_____ can order **62**_____ purple bracelets **63**_____ the organization **64**_____ one dollar **65**_____. So far, **66**_____ organization has **67**_____ out over **68**____ million bracelets **69**____ people all **70**_____ the world.

71____ few weeks **72**_____, our teacher **73**_____ us about **74**____ Complaint Free **75**_____, and we **76**_____ the article **77**_____ this organization. **78**_____ our class **79**_____ to try **80**_____ complaining for **81**_____ days. We **82**_____ the bracelets **83**_____, and they **84**_____ two days **85**_____. Since then, **86**_____ noticed how **87**_____ I complain. **88**_____ had to **89**_____ my bracelet **90**_____ one wrist **91**____ the other **92**____ least three **93**_____ every day! **94**_____ I'm doing **95**_____ today. I've **96**_____ had to **97**_____ my bracelet **98**_____ so far.

Listening Test 🕘 09:56

PART I: Picture Description (((Track 204)))

Listen and choose the statement that best describes what you see in the picture.

1.

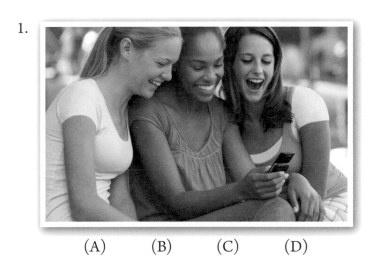

(A)   (B)   (C)   (D)

2.

(A)   (B)   (C)   (D)

3.

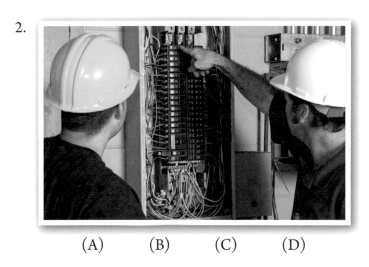

(A)   (B)   (C)   (D)

4.

(A)   (B)   (C)   (D)

5.

(A)   (B)   (C)   (D)

PART II: Questions and Responses ((Track 205))

Listen and choose the best response to each question.

6. (A)   (B)   (C)

7. (A)   (B)   (C)

8. (A)   (B)   (C)

9. (A)   (B)   (C)

10. (A)   (B)   (C)

PART III: Short Conversations ((Track 206))

You will hear two dialogs, each followed by three questions. Listen carefully, and choose the best answer to each question.

11. How would you describe the woman's feeling about losing her job?

    (A) She feels quite bad.
    (B) She is happy.
    (C) She was furious at first, but not anymore.
    (D) She does not feel too bad.

12. How does the man expect Joan to feel?

    (A) Upset
    (B) Joyful
    (C) Positive
    (D) Hopeful

13. What do you think the woman will do now?

    (A) She will feel sorry for herself.
    (B) She will try to have a better attitude.
    (C) She will try to find another job.
    (D) She will talk to more friends.

14. How does the woman feel?

    (A) Encouraged
    (B) Offended
    (C) Hopeful
    (D) Scared

15. Why did the man tell her to study something else?

    (A) He thinks she is not smart enough to study biology.
    (B) He wants her to take the same classes that he does.
    (C) He is a history major.
    (D) He thinks she would like history better.

16. How does the woman feel about studying biology?

    (A) It's just OK.
    (B) It's her favorite subject.
    (C) She doesn't like biology at all.
    (D) She has no feeling about it.

PART IV: Short Talks (((Track 207)))

You will hear two talks, each followed by three questions. Listen carefully, and choose the best answer to each question.

17. Which situation does this advice apply to?

    (A) Your friend feels sad about something.
    (B) You get upset by someone's comment.
    (C) A large group of people want to complain.
    (D) You upset someone by your comment to him or her.

18. What is the first piece of advice?

    (A) Be slow to speak.
    (B) Talk about your feelings.
    (C) React before the situation changes.
    (D) Avoid feelings of anger.

19. What is the second piece of advice?

    (A) Stay away from offensive people.
    (B) Keep personal comments to yourself.
    (C) Only give advice to people who ask first.
    (D) Think before you speak.

---

20. Who is the speaker upset with?

    (A) Her friend, Art
    (B) Her teacher
    (C) Her classmates
    (D) Her parents

21. According to the speaker, what is true about Art?

    (A) He always picks on her.
    (B) He makes her feel good.
    (C) He never notices her.
    (D) He doesn't know that she is telling the truth.

22. What can be inferred about the speaker?

    (A) She has feelings for Art.
    (B) She plans to avoid Art for a while.
    (C) She is going to speak to her teacher about her classmates.
    (D) She thinks the situation is a little funny.

Favors

Warm-up

A
Look & Listen

Listen to the dialogs. Write the number next to the object mentioned by the speakers. ((Track 208))

B
Listen Again

Listen again, and fill in the blanks. ((Track 209))

1. _____ asked _____ to _____ .
2. _____ asked _____ to _____ .
3. _____ asked _____ to _____ .
4. _____ asked _____ to _____ .

C
Essential Expressions

Write the words and phrases in order to make correct questions.

1. a favor? / ask you / Can I _____
2. a favor / Could you / do / for me? _____
3. me / do / Could you / a favor? _____
4. for me? / Could you / do / possibly / something _____
5. a really big / Can you / do / favor / for me? _____
6. a / Could / do / favor? / huge / me / you _____
7. a favor / ask / Could I / of you? _____
8. you / me / Could I / to do / ask / a favor? _____
9. help / I / if / you could / me. / was wondering _____
10. you / with / something? / me / help / Could _____

Listening Practice

A

How would you answer?

Listen. Write the answer. ((Track 210))

> I'd be glad to.   I kind of like the red one.   They look like they are.
> No problem. I'll be right back.   Just check to see if the door is locked.

1. _____
2. _____
3. _____
4. _____
5. _____

B

How would you ask?

Listen. Write the question. ((Track 211))

> Could you do me a huge favor?   Can you help me carry these?
> Would you deliver this parcel for me?   Should I cut my hair short?
> Should I keep your dinner warm in the oven?

1. _____
2. _____
3. _____
4. _____
5. _____

C

Picture Description

Describe the picture using the words below.

assisting	fixing
one of the pedals	upside down

_____
_____
_____

✓ **Listen to the description of the picture.** ((Track 212))

Speaking Practice

A

Pronunciation Practice

In casual speech, you may hear the phrase "what are you" pronounced as "whacha."

Written	Spoken
1. What are you doing with the remote control? 2. What are you looking at? 3. What are you studying for?	1. Whacha doin' with the remote control? 2. Whacha looking at? 3. Whacha studying for?

✓ **Now practice saying the following sentences.**

1. What are you watching?
2. What are you making?
3. What are you going to do now?

✓ **Now listen and repeat.** ((Track 213))

B

Conversation Pictures

Listen to the dialogs, and number the pictures. ((Track 214))

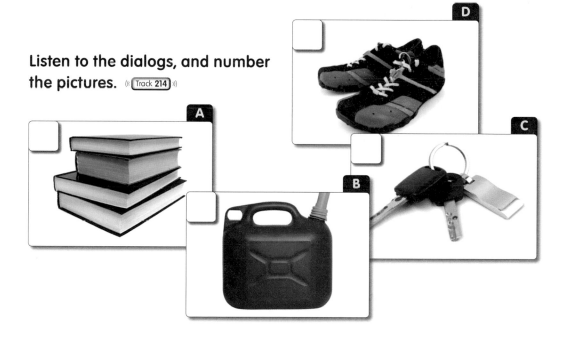

✓ **Now listen to the dialogs again, and choose the favor mentioned by the speakers.**

1. (A) Carry something (B) Go shopping (C) Return to store (D) Use phone
2. (A) Carry something (B) Go shopping (C) Return to store (D) Use phone
3. (A) Carry something (B) Go shopping (C) Return to store (D) Use phone
4. (A) Carry something (B) Go shopping (C) Return to store (D) Use phone

Short Dialogs

Listen to the dialog and questions. Choose the best answer. ((Track 215))

1. (A) A broken window   (B) Her fear of storms
   (C) Missing dinner   (D) Rain

2. (A) Borrow the car   (B) Go outside
   (C) Open a window   (D) Open the oven

✓ Listen again, and fill in the blanks.

M: Was that ❶_____ that I just heard?

W: I think so. It's getting really ❷_____ outside.
    I think it's going to start ❸_____ soon.

M: Uh, oh. Can you look out the window and see if my car
    ❹_____ are rolled up?

W: It looks like one of your ❺_____ windows is
    rolled down.

M: Can you do a really big ❻_____ for me? I need
    to check the chicken in the ❼_____. Could you
    run out there and ❽_____ my windows for me?

W: OK. I'll be right back.

Listen to the dialog and questions. Choose the best answer. ((Track 216))

1. (A) Boss and employee   (B) Husband and wife
   (C) Strangers   (D) Teacher and student

2. (A) Arrive by 8:00   (B) Bring the kids home
   (C) Go to a meeting   (D) Pick up a sandwich

Listen to the dialog, and complete each statement. ((Track 217))

1. _____ told _____ that she might have forgotten
   _____.

2. _____ asked _____ to see if _____
   _____.

Main Dialog

Listen to the dialog, and choose the best answer. ((Track 218))

1. What does the woman ask the man to tell her?
   - (A) A good brand name
   - (B) A popular gift
   - (C) His favorite color
   - (D) His shirt size

2. What information does the man say she needs?
   - (A) His arm length
   - (B) His chest size
   - (C) His height
   - (D) His neck size

3. Why couldn't the woman go home for the information?
   - (A) Her husband has the car.
   - (B) She doesn't have a tape measure.
   - (C) She lives far away.
   - (D) The store will close.

Listen again, and fill in the blanks. ((Track 219))

M: Good morning, ma'am. ❶_____ I help you?

W: I'm looking for a ❷_____ gift for my husband, but I'm having some trouble. ❸_____ I ask you a favor?

M: Certainly. How ❹_____ I help you?

W: You're about the same ❺_____ as my husband. Could you tell me your ❻_____ size?

M: I wear a medium. However, all of these shirts have slightly different ❼_____ sizes as well. To get the right shirt for your husband, you really ❽_____ to know his neck size.

W: It is probably the same as ❾_____. What is your neck size?

M: I don't know that off the top of my head, ma'am. But let me get a ❿_____ measure and we can find out.

W: It's very kind of you to do all of this for me. I would have just gone home and found one of my husband's shirts, but I live about ⓫_____ minutes away from here.

M: It's no trouble at all, ma'am. According to this tape measure, my neck size is ⓬_____.

Short Talks

Listen to the short talk and questions. Choose the best answer. ((Track 220))

1. (A) Knowledge
   (B) Money
   (C) Strength
   (D) Time

2. (A) He did this favor for his friend.
   (B) He hasn't asked his friend yet.
   (C) His friend said no.
   (D) His friend said yes.

✓ **Listen again, and fill in the blanks.**

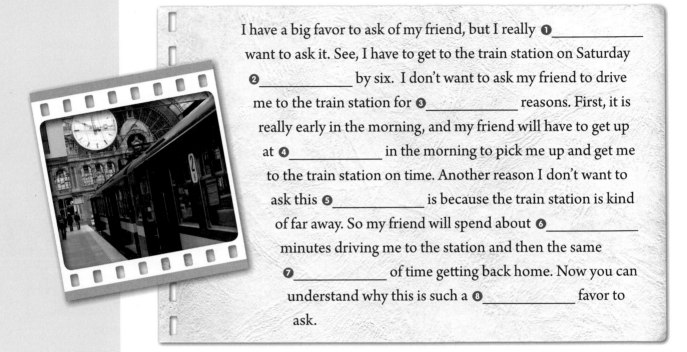

I have a big favor to ask of my friend, but I really ❶_____ want to ask it. See, I have to get to the train station on Saturday ❷_____ by six. I don't want to ask my friend to drive me to the train station for ❸_____ reasons. First, it is really early in the morning, and my friend will have to get up at ❹_____ in the morning to pick me up and get me to the train station on time. Another reason I don't want to ask this ❺_____ is because the train station is kind of far away. So my friend will spend about ❻_____ minutes driving me to the station and then the same ❼_____ of time getting back home. Now you can understand why this is such a ❽_____ favor to ask.

Listen to the short talk and questions. Choose the best answer. ((Track 221))

1. (A) Carmen
   (B) Elizabeth
   (C) Elizabeth's mom
   (D) Wanda

2. (A) Give someone a message
   (B) Have breakfast together
   (C) Meet after ballet class
   (D) Pick her up for school

Listen to the short talk, and write T for true or F for false for each statement. ((Track 222))

1. _____ The speaker wants to join the school's track team.
2. _____ The speaker enjoys weight lifting, jogging, and playing tennis.

Listening Quiz

04:52

Listen to the dialogs. Choose the correct picture. ((Track 223))

A

B

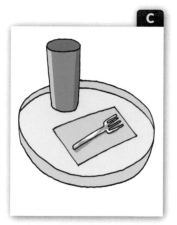

C

1. (A)   (B)   (C)

2. (A)   (B)   (C)

Listen to the dialogs and questions. Choose the best answer. ((Track 224))

3. (A) Call Bright Electronics   (B) Fix the woman's computer
   (C) Give someone a message   (D) Pick up the shipment

4. (A) For him to buy the dress   (B) For him to cut the tag off
   (C) For him to fix the zipper   (D) For him to give her some scissors

5. (A) Pink roses   (B) White lilies
   (C) Both lilies and roses   (D) Neither lilies nor roses

6. (A) Bake something   (B) Crack the nuts
   (C) Go to the store   (D) Pay for breakfast

7. (A) Classmates   (B) Colleagues
   (C) Family   (D) Neighbors

8. (A) Mr. Kim's house   (B) The airport
   (C) The fifth floor   (D) The parking garage

9. (A) Call a cab for her   (B) Drive her to the airport
   (C) Give the parcel to her   (D) Park the car for her

Wrap-up

A Pre-listening Discussion

Talk about these questions.

1. If you asked to borrow a stranger's cell phone, do you think he or she would let you?
2. If you asked ten people to fill out a survey, how many would do it?
3. If someone asked for help getting to a place you know, would you help him or her?

B Listening Comprehension

Listen and answer the questions. Track 225

1. **Who is Franck Flynn?**

____

2. **In Flynn's research, did more or fewer people help than expected?**

____

3. **In Flynn's research, what happened when people used the word "favor"?**

____

C Dictation Practice

Listen again, and fill in the blanks. Track 226

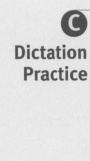

Researchers who ① ____ people have ② ____ up with ③ ____ clever ways ④ ____ study favors. ⑤ ____ information collected ⑥ ____ these studies ⑦ ____ us interesting ⑧ ____ about the ⑨ ____ people think ⑩ ____ favors.

One ⑪ ____ the most ⑫ ____ studies was ⑬ ____ by a ⑭ ____ of business ⑮ ____ Stanford University. ⑯ ____ professor's name ⑰ ____ Franck Flynn. ⑱ ____ the study ⑲ ____ he set ⑳ ____, Flynn found ㉑ ____ couple of ㉒ ____ things. First, ㉓ ____ found that ㉔ ____ people think ㉕ ____ generally don't ㉖ ____ to help ㉗ ____. How did ㉘ ____ figure this ㉙ ____? He asked ㉚ ____ people who ㉛ ____ helping in ㉜ ____ research to ㉝ ____ how many ㉞ ____ they would ㉟ ____ to ask ㊱ ____ a favor. ㊲ ____ example, he ㊳ ____ his helpers ㊴ ____ guess how ㊵ ____ people out ㊶ ____ ten or ㊷ ____ would agree ㊸ ____ do a ㊹ ____. The kinds ㊺ ____ favors in ㊻ ____ study were ㊼ ____ like filling ㊽ ____ a survey, ㊾ ____ a cell ㊿ ____, or guiding (51) ____ to some (52) ____ on campus. (53) ____ favor-askers (54) ____ guessed that (55) ____ would have (56) ____ ask a (57) ____ of people (58) ____ they found (59) ____ certain number (60) ____ would say (61) ____. But they (62) ____ wrong. After (63) ____ the research, (64) ____ favor-askers (65) ____ that a (66) ____ more people (67) ____ yes than (68) ____ thought.

Another (69) ____ thing that (70) ____ found in (71) ____ research was (72) ____ power of (73) ____ word "favor." (74) ____ using that (75) ____ seemed to (76) ____ it more (77) ____ for people (78) ____ agree to (79) ____. For example, (80) ____ the asker (81) ____ asked people (82) ____ fill out (83) ____ survey, only (84) ____ percent of (85) ____ people agreed (86) ____ do it. (87) ____ then Flynn (88) ____ his helpers (89) ____ change the (90) ____. He told (91) ____ to ask (92) ____, "Can you (93) ____ me a (94) ____ and fill (95) ____ this survey?" (96) ____ the helpers (97) ____ that, over (98) ____ percent of (99) ____ people agreed (100) ____ do it!

Listening Test ⏱ 09:49

PART I: Picture Description ((Track 227))

Listen and choose the statement that best describes what you see in the picture.

1.

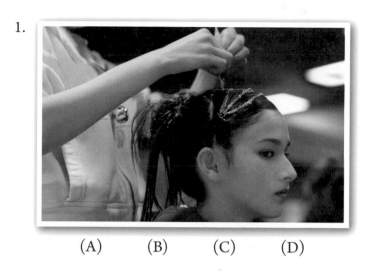

(A)   (B)   (C)   (D)

2.

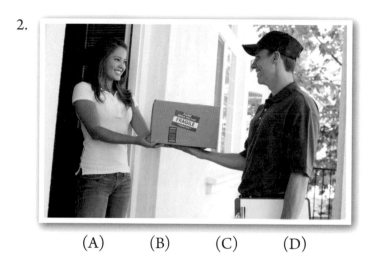

(A)   (B)   (C)   (D)

3.

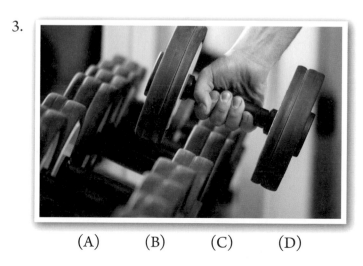

(A)   (B)   (C)   (D)

4.

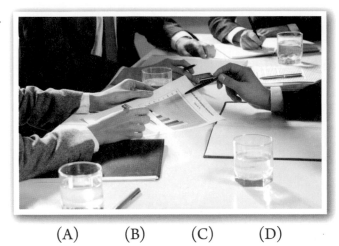

(A)　　　(B)　　　(C)　　　(D)

5.

(A)　　　(B)　　　(C)　　　(D)

PART II: Questions and Responses ((Track 228))

Listen and choose the best response to each question.

6. (A)　　　(B)　　　(C)

7. (A)　　　(B)　　　(C)

8. (A)　　　(B)　　　(C)

9. (A)　　　(B)　　　(C)

10. (A)　　　(B)　　　(C)

PART III: Short Conversations ((Track 229))

You will hear two dialogs, each followed by three questions. Listen carefully, and choose the best answer to each question.

11. What occasion are the speakers preparing for?

    (A) A concert

    (B) A meal

    (C) A party

    (D) A wedding

12. What does the man suggest at first?

    (A) Wearing the black dress

    (B) Wearing the blue dress

    (C) Wearing the most expensive dress

    (D) Wearing the red dress

13. Why does the woman choose the black dress?

    (A) To look like the others

    (B) To look slimmer and taller

    (C) To please the man

    (D) To save time

---

14. What does Mary offer to do for the man?

    (A) Make some soup

    (B) Get groceries

    (C) Put the juice away

    (D) Finish his work

15. Why does Mary offer to help the man?

    (A) He is tired.

    (B) He doesn't like to go to the store.

    (C) He is sick.

    (D) He likes to drink lots of liquids.

16. What will the man do while Mary does the favor?

    (A) He will rest.

    (B) He will go to the store.

    (C) He will have some juice.

    (D) He will ask for more help.

PART IV: Short Talks ((Track 230))

You will hear two talks, each followed by three questions. Listen carefully, and choose the best answer to each question.

17. How does the man feel about asking for favors?

(A) He doesn't like asking for advice.
(B) He thinks it is a good idea.
(C) He usually feels nervous to ask for help.
(D) He is afraid his friend asks for favors too often.

18. What two factors might affect the decision to do someone a favor?

(A) Worry and advice
(B) Time and ability
(C) Friendship and personal space
(D) Thinking and asking

19. What is the final piece of advice suggested by the speaker?

(A) Ask in advance.
(B) Remember to return the favor.
(C) Surprise your friend.
(D) Don't be afraid to help.

---

20. What is the information about?

(A) Polite ways to avoid calls
(B) Writing quick notes
(C) Giving people useful information
(D) Leaving a message

21. What does the speaker suggest?

(A) Ask the person to read the message to you
(B) Tell the person what to write down
(C) Put the message in an easy-to-find place
(D) Don't give your phone number to strangers

22. Which of the following is NOT mentioned as important information?

(A) Address
(B) Name
(C) Time
(D) Phone number

UNIT 11 Memories

Warm-up

A
Look & Listen

Listen to the dialogs. Write the number next to the picture mentioned by the speakers. ((Track 231))

A ☐   B ☐   C ☐   D ☐

B
Listen Again

Listen again, and match the photo with the time it was taken. ((Track 232))

birthday	camping	vacation	wedding

1. _____ – last summer
2. _____ – while in California
3. _____ – a couple of years ago
4. _____ – last month

C
Essential Expressions

Write the irregular past and past perfect form of each verb or phrasal verb.

	Past	Past perfect
1. babysit	_____	have _____
2. buy	_____	have _____
3. take	_____	have _____
4. drive	_____	have _____
5. fly	_____	have _____
6. forget	_____	have _____
7. get married	_____	have _____
8. go camping	_____	have _____
9. leave	_____	have _____
10. swim	_____	have _____

Listening Practice

A

How would you answer?

Listen. Write the answer. ((Track 233))

It was awesome!	Sure, I do.	Yes, we all went.
We both ordered lobster.		They certainly were.

1. _____
2. _____
3. _____
4. _____
5. _____

Listen. Write the question. ((Track 234))

B

How would you ask?

Who did you go to dinner with?	What did you do there?
When did you last see them?	How did you enjoy it?
Remember that camping trip we went on?	

1. _____
2. _____
3. _____
4. _____
5. _____

C

Picture Description

Describe the picture using the words below.

admiring	album
ladies	photos

_____
_____
_____
_____

✓ **Listen to the description of the picture.** ((Track 235))

Speaking Practice

A

Intonation Practice

In certain four-syllable words, the stress will usually be on the first syllable. Study the following words that typically have the stress pattern "da dum dum dum."

Written	Spoken
1. baby-sitter	1. **ba**by-sitter
2. interesting	2. **in**teresting
3. definitely	3. **def**initely

✓ Now practice saying the following words. Remember to stress the first syllable.

1. January
2. dictionary
3. category

✓ **Now listen and repeat.** (((Track 236)))

B

Conversation Pictures

Listen to the dialogs, and number the pictures. (((Track 237)))

✓ **Now listen to the dialogs again, and choose the memory mentioned by the speakers.**

1. (A) Educational   (B) Embarrassing   (C) Fun   (D) Terrifying
2. (A) Educational   (B) Embarrassing   (C) Fun   (D) Terrifying
3. (A) Educational   (B) Embarrassing   (C) Fun   (D) Terrifying
4. (A) Educational   (B) Embarrassing   (C) Fun   (D) Terrifying

Short Dialogs

Listen to the dialog and questions. Choose the best answer. ((Track 238))

1. (A) The beach   (B) The drive
   (C) The food   (D) The weather

2. (A) He ate them.   (B) He has them.
   (C) They are gone.   (D) They were pretty.

✓ **Listen again, and fill in the blanks.**

W: Remember that winter vacation our whole family went
❶_____ in Florida?

M: Yeah, it was January when I was ❷_____ and
you were ten. It took three days to ❸_____
there from Chicago.

W: That was ❹_____ years ago. How come it took
so long to get there?

M: It had ❺_____ the day before we left, so a lot of
roads had been closed.

W: The thing I remember most about that vacation was that
we ❻_____ in the ocean every day.

M: I remember the ❼_____ bucket of seashells
that we collected. I wonder what ❽_____ to
all of those seashells.

Listen to the dialog, and questions. Choose the best answer. ((Track 239))

1. (A) A previous date   (B) A similar place
   (C) The restaurant's name   (D) The woman's order

2. (A) The man   (B) The woman
   (C) Both the man and the woman   (D) Neither the man nor the woman

Listen to the dialog, and choose the right word or phrase to complete each sentence. ((Track 240))

1. The woman got a ticket for not (going the right speed / using her signal).
2. This is the woman's (first / fourth) ticket.

Main Dialog

Listen to the dialog, and choose the best answer. ((Track 241))

1. What favor does Janet ask of Ned?
   - (A) Drive to Michigan
   - (B) Help her great-aunts
   - (C) Take care of her dog
   - (D) Watch her house

2. How long will Janet be gone?
   - (A) The weekend
   - (B) One week
   - (C) Two weeks
   - (D) One month

3. When did Janet last see her great-aunts?
   - (A) At a special event
   - (B) During the vacation
   - (C) As a very young child
   - (D) When she was eight

Listen again, and fill in the blanks. ((Track 242))

M: Morning, Janet. How's it going? Your ❶_____ is looking great.

W: Thanks. Ned's been working on it in his spare time. Listen, we ❷_____ to ask you and Maggie if you could do us a favor. Could you watch our ❸_____ while we're gone?

M: Sure. After all, what are ❹_____ for? Where are you two headed this time?

W: We're ❺_____ up to see my two great-aunts in Michigan. We're leaving tomorrow ❻_____.

M: How long will you be gone?

W: Two ❼_____. I'm sorry for the short notice, but I thought Ned had asked you last ❽_____. He just told me last night that he had forgotten to.

M: It's no problem. Maggie and I aren't going ❾_____. You said you're going to visit your great-aunts? How ❿_____ are they?

W: They're both in their ⓫_____. I haven't seen them since my sister's ⓬_____ about eight years ago.

Short Talks

Listen to the short talk and questions. Choose the best answer. (((Track 243)))

1. (A) George cooked dinner for her.   (B) Her husband took them all to dinner.
   (C) Her mother-in-law cooked dinner.   (D) She cooked for her mother-in-law.

2. (A) Bought a dictionary   (B) Lived with her mother-in-law
   (C) Studied and practiced   (D) Went to Mexico for three years

✓ **Listen again, and fill in the blanks.**

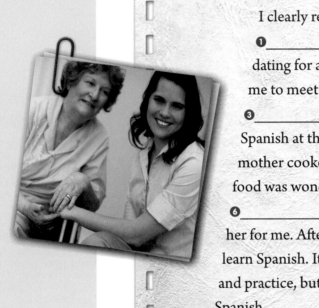

I clearly remember the first time that I met my husband's
❶_____. My husband, George, and I had only been
dating for a few ❷_____ at that time. Before he took
me to meet his mother, George warned me his mother didn't
❸_____ any English. Of course, I didn't speak any
Spanish at that time, so I was very ❹_____. George's
mother cooked dinner for us that ❺_____, and the
food was wonderful. I really wanted to tell her how much I had
❻_____ the meal, but I could only ask George to tell
her for me. After that night, I ❼_____ that I would
learn Spanish. It took me about three years of ❽_____
and practice, but at least now I can have a basic conversation in
Spanish.

Listen to the short talk and questions. Choose the best answer. (((Track 244)))

1. (A) A romantic evening   (B) An embarrassing time
   (C) An exciting game   (D) An interesting trip

2. (A) He asked his friend for help.   (B) He became more careful.
   (C) He planned to be a police officer.   (D) He stopped making the signs.

Listen to the short talk, and circle three things that the twins did. (((Track 245)))

built a tent   rode bikes   played computer games

read books   made a mess   watched a video

A
Picture Matching

Listen to the dialogs. Choose the correct picture. ((Track 246))

A

B

C

1. (A)   (B)   (C)

2. (A)   (B)   (C)

B
Listen & Choose

Listen to the dialogs and questions. Choose the best answer. ((Track 247))

3. (A) Famous people   (B) Her in-laws
   (C) His ancestors   (D) The young generation

4. (A) The man   (B) The woman
   (C) Both the man and the woman   (D) Neither the man nor the woman

5. (A) A relative sent them.   (B) He bought them.
   (C) People collected them.   (D) She found them.

6. (A) All of them   (B) Some of them
   (C) Only one of them   (D) None of them

7. (A) He did not sing.   (B) He enjoys her jokes.
   (C) He sang with the woman.   (D) He went there many times.

8. (A) They are twins.   (B) They are younger than the man.
   (C) They had the same kind of job.   (D) They have always lived together.

9. (A) Becoming teachers   (B) Living so long
   (C) Never marrying   (D) Taking the photo together

Wrap-up

A Pre-listening Discussion

Talk about these questions.

1. How do you memorize people's names?
2. How do you memorize English vocabulary?
3. How do you memorize math formulas?

B Listening Comprehension

Listen and answer the questions. (Track 248)

1. **What is the first rule for memorizing something?**

   ____

2. **How many pieces of information can a person's short term memory hold?**

   ____

3. **What suggestion does the speaker give for memorizing a long number?**

   ____

C Dictation Practice

Listen again, and fill in the blanks. (Track 249)

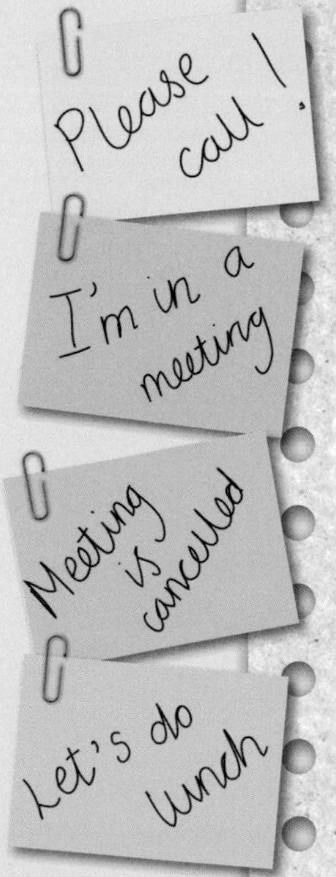

Please call!
I'm in a meeting
Meeting is cancelled
Let's do lunch

In my ❶________ and math ❷________, I always ❸________ to memorize ❹________ of things ❺______ science and ❻______ kinds of ❼________ formulas. Since ❽____ memory is ❾______ that great, ❿______ had to ⓫________ ways to ⓬__________ my memory. ⓭________ you could ⓮________ from some ⓯____ the tips ⓰________ I've picked ⓱____ for memorizing ⓲________. Or maybe ⓳______ already do ⓴________ things anyway.

㉑____ course, the ㉒________ rule of ㉓____________ something is ㉔____ repeat it. ㉕______ can repeat ㉖____ out loud ㉗____ you can ㉘________ repeat it ㉙____ your mind. ㉚______ example, on ㉛______ first day ㉜____ class, sometimes ㉝______ teacher will ㉞______ all the ㉟__________ to introduce ㊱____________. I use ㊲________ class time ㊳____ a chance ㊴____ exercise my ㊵__________ skills. As ㊶____ go around ㊷______ room, I ㊸______ to memorize ㊹________ student's name ㊺____ repeating his or her name ㊻____ myself. Most ㊼____ the time, ㊽____ the end ㊾____ class, I ㊿________ memorized everyone's (51)________.

Another trick (52)____ have learned (53)______ memorizing things (54)____ to build (55)____ small pieces (56)____ order to (57)________ longer things. (58)________ idea comes (59)________ the fact (60)________ a person's (61)________ term memory (62)______ only hold (63)________ or nine (64)________ of information (65)____ a time. (66)____ those pieces (67)____ information in (68)________ term memory (69)________ to be (70)________ to long (71)________ memory by (72)__________ them again (73)______ again before (74)________ information can (75)____ into short (76)________ memory. Another (77)________ related to (78)________ idea is (79)____ put larger "(80)________" of information (81)________ short term (82)__________.

Here is (83)____ example of (84)________ I mean. (85)______ you want (86)____ memorize the (87)__________ 9893512276. You (88)________ try to (89)____________ each number (90)____ itself. Or, (91)____ better idea (92)________ be to (93)____________ the numbers (94)____ groups like (95)________-351-22-(96)______.

Listening Test 🕙 10:27

PART I: Picture Description (((Track 250)))

Listen and choose the statement that best describes what you see in the picture.

1.

(A)   (B)   (C)   (D)

2.

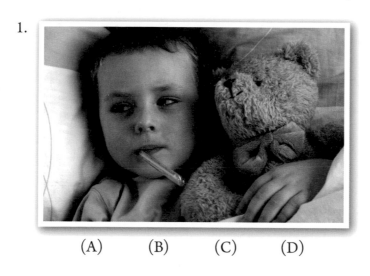

(A)   (B)   (C)   (D)

3.

(A)   (B)   (C)   (D)

4.

(A)   (B)   (C)   (D)

5.

(A)   (B)   (C)   (D)

PART II: Questions and Responses ((Track 251))

Listen and choose the best response to each question.

6. (A)   (B)   (C)

7. (A)   (B)   (C)

8. (A)   (B)   (C)

9. (A)   (B)   (C)

10. (A)   (B)   (C)

PART III: Short Conversations ((Track 252))

You will hear two dialogs, each followed by three questions. Listen carefully, and choose the best answer to each question.

11. What are the man and woman talking about?

    (A) The woman's first bike
    (B) How the woman likes to ride bikes
    (C) The easiest way to learn how to ride a bike
    (D) The woman's first experience riding a bike

12. When did the woman learn to do this activity?

    (A) Whenever she was at home
    (B) Before she was six years old
    (C) Any time that she was with her dad
    (D) When she wanted to go outside

13. What helped the woman learn to do this activity quickly?

    (A) Training wheels
    (B) Talking to her dad
    (C) Advice from a friend
    (D) Telling the man about it

---

14. What did the woman find?

    (A) A picture of her with her mom and dad
    (B) Her aunt's wedding dress
    (C) A photo album
    (D) A special toy from her childhood

15. Where did the woman find it?

    (A) In her toy box
    (B) At her parents' house
    (C) In a drawer
    (D) With the man

16. What memory does it bring back to the woman?

    (A) Playing dress up
    (B) Flowers in the garden
    (C) Moving to a new house
    (D) Her aunt's wedding

PART IV: Short Talks ((Track 253))

You will hear two talks, each followed by three questions. Listen carefully, and choose the best answer to each question.

17. What is the man's memory about?

    (A) Being nervous in front of crowds
    (B) Learning to play baseball
    (C) What a coach did to him
    (D) His first bad experience in life

18. What happened when the coach hit the ball?

    (A) It landed on his head.
    (B) The speaker started to cry.
    (C) The coach laughed at him.
    (D) The speaker had to go to the outfield.

19. What did the boy learn from this experience?

    (A) How to play baseball
    (B) When to play in the outfield
    (C) Why crying never helps
    (D) How to be strong

20. Which is NOT true about the summer that the speaker remembers?

    (A) Her grandfather was at her house.
    (B) The temperature was very high.
    (C) They put a roof on the house.
    (D) Her grandfather was sick.

21. What did the speaker's grandfather teach her how to do?

    (A) Be safe in hurricanes
    (B) Use tools
    (C) Recognize a good roof
    (D) Take care of small injuries

22. How does the speaker remember the experience?

    (A) As scary
    (B) As embarrassing
    (C) As a good time
    (D) As too much work

UNIT 12 Assistance

Warm-up

A
Look & Listen

Listen to the dialogs. Write the number next to the speakers. ((Track 254))

B
Listen Again

Listen again, and fill in the blanks. ((Track 255))

1. The student needs help _____ .
2. The woman needs help _____ .
3. The student needs help _____ .
4. The girl needs help _____ .

C
Essential Expressions

Circle the best word or phrase to complete each question.

1. (Can / May) you walk me to the door of the building?
2. If your teacher agrees, then I (can / could) put you on the list.
3. (May / Would) I interrupt you for a minute?
4. The nurse said I (can't / might) lift anything heavy.
5. Were you (able to / could) help her with her homework?
6. Is there any way that I (can / should) turn it in late?
7. (Be able to / Could) I get the phone number from you?
8. (Did / Would) you help them with their chores yesterday?
9. I (can't / couldn't) do it right now, but maybe later.
10. (Won't / Would) you like me to give you a hand with those?

Listening Practice

A

How would you answer?

Listen. Write the answer. ((Track 256))

That's all right. I can get it.　　　Not at all.　　　Could I? Thanks!
Which office do you mean?　　　Sorry. I don't know much about them.

1. _____
2. _____
3. _____
4. _____
5. _____

B

How would you ask?

Listen. Write the question. ((Track 257))

Can you give me a hand with this box?　　　Would you like me to go with you?
You'll be able to help me, won't you?　　　Should I close the window for you?
　　　　　Could you help me solve these problems?

1. _____
2. _____
3. _____
4. _____
5. _____

C

Picture Description

Describe the picture using the words below.

hanging	holding
outdoors	playground

_____
_____
_____
_____

✓ **Listen to the description of the picture.** ((Track 258))

Speaking Practice

A
Pronunciation Practice

In casual speech, you may hear the phrase "got you" pronounced as "gotcha."

Written	Spoken
1. I got you. (I understand.)	1. I gotcha.
2. Got you! (Tricked or fooled you!)	2. Gotcha!
3. I got you a sandwich for lunch.	3. I gotcha a sandwich for lunch.

✓ **Now practice saying the following sentences.**

1. They got you good with that trick.
2. I got you something.
3. Oh, I got you, it's in the blue box.

✓ **Now listen and repeat.** ((Track 259))

B
Conversation Pictures

Listen to the dialogs, and number the pictures. ((Track 260))

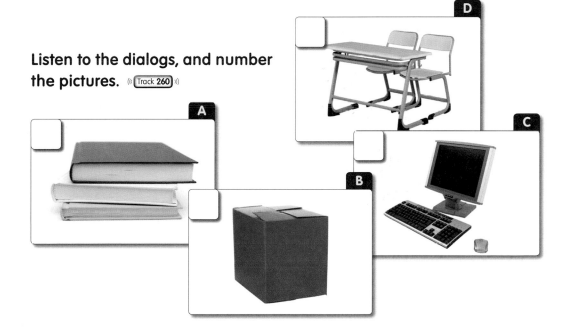

✓ **Now listen to the dialogs again, and check (✓) what the person does or will do in each conversation.**

1. Woman: ☐ will pay   ☐ won't pay
2. Woman: ☐ moves it   ☐ doesn't move it
3. Man: ☐ checks it   ☐ doesn't check it
4. Man: ☐ carries   ☐ doesn't carry

Short Dialogs

A

Dialog 1

Listen to the dialog and questions. Choose the best answer. ((Track 261))

1. (A) It is not allowed in the office.   (B) She will be at the meeting.
   (C) She won't be at her desk.   (D) The phone won't work.

2. (A) Call back tomorrow   (B) Call her cell phone number
   (C) Call the man's number   (D) When to call again

✓ **Listen again, and fill in the blanks.**

M: Cathy, I've got to go to a ❶_____. Can I transfer my calls to your number?

W: You ❷_____, but I'll only be here for about ❸_____ more minutes.

M: Oh, then I'll ask Ellen if we can ❹_____ transfer our calls to her.

W: I ❺_____ do that. I'm supposed to ❻_____ all my calls.

M: How do you do that when you're ❼_____ here?

W: I leave a message with my ❽_____ number.

B

Dialog 2

Listen to the dialog and questions. Choose the best answer. ((Track 262))

1. (A) She dislikes driving at night.   (B) She doesn't know how to drive.
   (C) She only drives short distances.   (D) She won't be allowed to drive.

2. (A) He can't help her.   (B) He may be able to help.
   (C) He wants her to help him.   (D) He will definitely help her.

C

Dialog 3

Listen to the dialog, and choose the right word to complete each sentence. ((Track 263))

1. The man (can't / might / will) list Ms. Jacobs as a reference.
2. The woman (may / will / won't) give him a phone number to list for her.

Main Dialog

Listen to the dialog, and choose the best answer. ((Track 264))

1. Most likely, what is the relationship of the speakers?
   - (A) Brother and sister
   - (B) Co-workers
   - (C) Husband and wife
   - (D) Neighbors

2. Which is true about the books that the man has?
   - (A) He borrowed them.
   - (B) He bought them.
   - (C) He wrote them.
   - (D) He plans to give them away.

3. What did the woman help the man with?
   - (A) Finding the books
   - (B) Closing the door of the building
   - (C) Using the elevator
   - (D) Opening his apartment door

Listen again, and fill in the blanks. ((Track 265))

W: Can I get that ❶_____ for you?

M: Oh, yes, thank you! I was wondering how I was going to ❷_____ it.

W: There you go. Are you headed ❸_____?

M: Actually, yes. I live on the ❹_____ floor.

W: Let me get the ❺_____ for you. You said the fifth floor, right?

M: Right. Thanks for all the help.

W: Don't mention it. What are all those ❻_____ for, anyway? Sorry. Am I being too nosy?

M: Not at all. I guess it must ❼_____ like I just came from a huge book ❽_____ or something.

W: I'm guessing those are ❾_____ books. I can see the book numbers on some of them.

M: You have a good eye. I'm doing some reading for a ❿_____ paper. You are looking at my plans for the ⓫_____ right here.

W: I see. Oh, here is my ⓬_____. Good luck with your research.

M: Thanks. And thanks again for your help.

Short Talks

Short Talk 1

Listen to the short talk and questions. Choose the best answer. ((Track 266))

1. (A) He tried to help someone.   (B) Someone tried to help him.
   (C) They both tried to help someone.   (D) Someone tried to help both of them.

2. (A) The speaker   (B) His friend
   (C) A classmate   (D) No one

✓ **Listen again, and fill in the blanks.**

We have a big paper due in ❶_____ class at the end
of the week. I've been having some trouble ❷_____
the paper, so for the past couple of days I've been skipping
❸_____ to work on it. Yesterday, a friend of mine found
me in the ❹_____ and sat beside me. He told me, "I got
you a ❺_____ for lunch." Then he handed it to me, along
with an orange. That was awfully nice of him. Unfortunately, he
brought me a ❻_____ sandwich. I'm allergic to
peanuts, so I ❼_____ eat it. I told my friend I would get
something to drink later and eat the sandwich on my way to class.
Really, I had to just ❽_____ it away.

Short Talk 2

Listen to the short talk and questions. Choose the best answer. ((Track 267))

1. (A) To borrow something   (B) To join the team
   (C) To look for something   (D) To win the competition

2. (A) She feels proud.   (B) She is glad she could help.
   (C) She regrets helping.   (D) She is relieved it is finished.

Short Talk 3

Listen to the short talk, and match two phrases to each person. ((Track 268))

1. Started the club •   • The speaker •   • 3. Was behind schedule

2. Joined the club •   • His friend •   • 4. Made an audio CD

A

Picture Matching

Listen to the dialogs. Choose the correct picture. ((Track 269))

 **A**

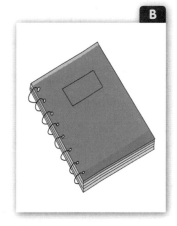 **B**

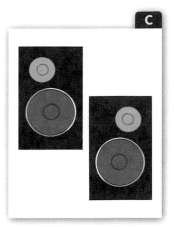 **C**

1. (A)   (B)   (C)

2. (A)   (B)   (C)

B

Listen & Choose

Listen to the dialogs and questions. Choose the best answer. ((Track 270))

3. (A) Driving at night   (B) Finding a movie
   (C) Knowing the time   (D) Watching children

4. (A) He already did it for her.   (B) He can't do it for her.
   (C) He might do it for her.   (D) He will do it for her.

5. (A) Choosing a picture   (B) Cleaning the dining room
   (C) Holding a picture   (D) Moving to the apartment

6. (A) Broadway   (B) Campus
   (C) The library   (D) The woman's house

7. (A) It is not a problem for her. (B) It is not certain that she can help.
   (C) It is out of the way for her. (D) It is too early for her.

8. (A) Borrow a book   (B) Copy her notes
   (C) See his professor   (D) Use a machine

9. (A) The librarian   (B) The student
   (C) The professor   (D) The secretary

Wrap-up

A
Pre-listening Discussion

Talk about these questions.

1. Would you help someone even if they didn't ask for help?
2. If you see other people helping someone, would you offer to help, too?
3. Can you retell the story of the Good Samaritan? If so, tell it.

B
Listening Comprehension

Listen and answer the questions. Track 271

1. **What are the two theories described by the speaker?**

   ____

2. **What kind of thought may make a bystander choose not to help someone?**

   ____

3. **Who do Good Samaritans tend to pay attention to in situations where help is needed?**

   ____

C
Dictation Practice

Listen again, and fill in the blanks. Track 272

The story ①____ the Good Samaritan ②____ about a ③____ from another ④____ stopping to ⑤____ a complete ⑥____. Not only ⑦____ the Good Samaritan ⑧____ to help, ⑨____ he went ⑩____ of his ⑪____ to help ⑫____ stranger, even ⑬____ for the ⑭____ to stay ⑮____ a safe ⑯____ until the ⑰____ was well ⑱____ to travel.

⑲____ psychology, there ⑳____ a theory ㉑____ why people ㉒____ in helpful ㉓____, called the ㉔____ Samaritan effect. ㉕____, there are ㉖____ theories to ㉗____ the way ㉘____ act: the ㉙____ Samaritan effect ㉚____ the bystander ㉛____. A bystander ㉜____ a person ㉝____ sees a ㉞____ but just ㉟____ and watches. ㊱____ bystander doesn't ㊲____ in to ㊳____, whereas the ㊴____ Samaritan jumps ㊵____ to lend ㊶____ hand.

When ㊷____ study these ㊸____ effects, they ㊹____ to explain ㊺____ by the ㊻____ ways people ㊼____. For example, ㊽____ person may ㊾____ may not ㊿____ in some (51)____, depending on (52)____ the person (53)____ others to (54)____ him. A (55)____ may not (56)____ because he (57)____ want to (58)____ foolish by (59)____ a mistake (60)____ trying to (61)____ out. On (62)____ other hand, (63)____ Good Samaritan (64)____ choose to (65)____ because he (66)____ others to (67)____ how helpful (68)____ person he (69)____. In addition, (70)____ person may (71)____ may not (72)____ based on (73)____ he sees (74)____ doing. A (75)____ pays more (76)____ to other (77)____. If he (78)____ others who (79)____ helping, he (80)____ help, either. (81)____ Good Samaritan (82)____ attention to (83)____ Good Samaritans. (84)____ he sees (85)____ helping, he (86)____ encouraged to (87)____ as well.

(88)____ you have (89)____ or maybe (90)____ been in (91)____ with bystanders (92)____ Good Samaritans. (93)____ you the (94)____ who needed (95)____ in that (96)____? If not, (97)____ you a (98)____ or a (99)____ Samaritan at (100)____ time?

Listening Test

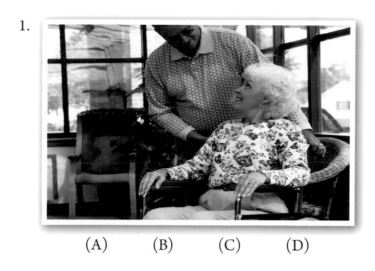

PART I: Picture Description ((Track 273))

Listen and choose the statement that best describes what you see in the picture.

1.

(A)   (B)   (C)   (D)

2.

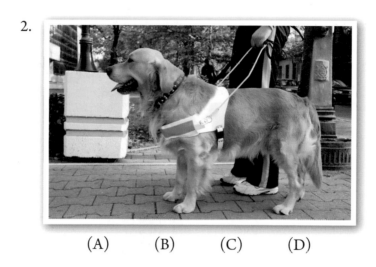

(A)   (B)   (C)   (D)

3.

(A)   (B)   (C)   (D)

4.

(A)   (B)   (C)   (D)

5.

(A)   (B)   (C)   (D)

PART II: Questions and Responses ((Track 274))

Listen and choose the best response to each question.

6. (A)   (B)   (C)

7. (A)   (B)   (C)

8. (A)   (B)   (C)

9. (A)   (B)   (C)

10. (A)   (B)   (C)

PART III: Short Conversations ((Track 275))

You will hear two dialogs, each followed by three questions. Listen carefully, and choose the best answer to each question.

11. What does the man need help with?

    (A) Turning it on
    (B) Giving copies to others
    (C) Fixing it
    (D) Finding the right page

12. What is wrong with the machine?

    (A) Something is stuck in it.
    (B) It has no power.
    (C) It is out of paper.
    (D) The door was not closed correctly.

13. Why does the woman tell the man to be careful?

    (A) Because it is not easy to help him
    (B) Because he might make the problem worse
    (C) Because there is some danger in reaching into the machine
    (D) Because the job can be very messy

---

14. What does the woman need help with?

    (A) Solving the problems
    (B) Learning the material
    (C) Naming molecules
    (D) Finding the chapter

15. What does the man offer to do?

    (A) Check her answers
    (B) Talk to the teacher
    (C) Explain the chapter
    (D) Meet her after class

16. When will the man help the woman?

    (A) After class
    (B) Right away
    (C) Tomorrow
    (D) Sometime in the future

PART IV: Short Talks ((Track 276))

You will hear two talks, each followed by three questions. Listen carefully, and choose the best answer to each question.

17. How often does the man say he helps strangers?

    (A) Only if he has extra time
    (B) Anytime they need help
    (C) Not very often
    (D) Whenever he notices

18. What was the woman's problem?

    (A) She didn't know which bus to take.
    (B) She wanted to go downtown.
    (C) She wasn't sure where she was.
    (D) She felt afraid of the people on the bus.

19. How did the man help the woman?

    (A) He told her which bus to take.
    (B) He told her where to get off the bus.
    (C) He calmed her down by saying nice things to her.
    (D) He thanked her.

---

20. Who asks the woman for advice?

    (A) Her friend
    (B) A neighbor
    (C) A family member
    (D) Her classmates

21. What is the first thing the woman does when she is asked for help?

    (A) She gives a solution.
    (B) She talks about her experience.
    (C) She suggests someone to talk to.
    (D) She asks what the person thinks of the problem.

22. How does the problem get resolved?

    (A) The person decides what's best.
    (B) The person and the woman decide what's best together.
    (C) The woman decides what's best by herself.
    (D) The whole family talks about it and decides what to do.